PAKISTAN UNDER ARMY RULE

M.M. Khajooria

GYAN

ISBN: 978-81-212-1199-4

Price: ₹ 760

First Published 2014

Published by

Gyan Publishing House
23, Main Ansari Road
Daryaganj, New Delhi-110002
Phones: 23282060, 23261060
Fax : 91-11-23285914
E-mail: books@gyanbooks.com
Laser Typesetting : Shah Computer Graphics
Printed at : G. Print Process, Delhi

Cataloging in Publication Data—DK
Courtesy: D.K. Agencies (P) Ltd. <docinfo@dkagencies.com>

Khajooria, M. M.
Pakistan under army rule / M.M. Khajooria.
p. cm.
Includes index.
ISBN 9788121211994

1. Pakistan—Politics and government—1988-
2. Musharraf, Pervez. 3. Pakistan Army—Political activity. 4. Military government—Pakistan.
5. Pakistan—Foreign relations. I. Title.

DDC 320.95491 23

The book is dedicated to the abiding memory of my wife

Madhu

Who made and enriched my life and quietly departed for the world beyond.

Contents

Preface

At the time of departure from the Indian Sub-continent, the British bequeathed upon the Dominions of India and Pakistan same structures for Constitution making and governance—a constituent assembly to draw up Constitution reflecting the will and aspirations of the people, which also duplicated as the Parliament, and legislative assemblies and Cabinets for the provinces. The permanent Civil Services and Defence forces were divided and assets identified and allocated to the two countries. Governor Generals were appointed to lend stability and continuity. Pakistan came into being on 14th of August, 1947; India had its "tryst with destiny" as Prime Minister Nehru put it on 15th August 1947. The governments at the centres and provinces were in place and constituent assemblies got down to their job in right earnest.

While India held the course, people gave themselves a Constitution proclaiming the country a secular, democratic republic wedded to the concept of a welfare state, Pakistan lost its way somewhere down the line. Superficially, the instability, confusion and lack of direction that became hall-marks of the new state may be explained as consequence of her birth pangs, colossal migration and blood bath, terminal ill health of Mohd. Ali Jinnah, the founding father and the first Governor

General resulting in his demise on 11 September, 1948 and assassination of Prime Minister Liaquat Ali Khan on 17 October, 1951. The roots of the misfortunes of that country, however, ran deeper embracing the political and hierarchal dynamics of Muslim League, lack of support for the very concept of Pakistan in the provinces that came to constitute the Dominion resulting in deficit of local leadership and talent for governance and inherent conflict between ethnicity and religion. The inevitable hurt of Punjabi pride and strong resentment against exclusion from top positions in the government of Pakistan generated its own pressures.

Ever since its creation about six and a half decades ago, Pakistan was ruled by Military Dictators for a total period of around thirty four years punctuated by spells of democratically elected government. Tragically, the elected governments with the exception of the government headed by Mr. Zulfikar Ali Bhutto (1971-77) were either the creation of army, or survived at the pleasure of its own chief of Army Staff. Significantly, Bhutto was not only dethroned but also "judicially executed" by his "favourite" chief of the Army Staff, General Zia- ul Haq, whom he had chosen over the heads of his seniors.

Contrary to public perception,the first person to subvert the Constitution and usurp the state power was not an Army General but a former Indian Accounts Service officer and Finance Minister in Liaquat Ali cabinet, Malik Ghulam Mohd., a Punjabi steeped in "Lahori culture." He had served the Nawab of Bhawalpur and Nizam of Hyderabad and was well-versed in the art of palace intrigues. Tipped to take over as Prime Minister on the assassination of Liaquat Ail Khan, he manoeuvred to persuade Governor General Nazim-ud-Din to 'voluntarily' opt for the post of Prime Minister and thus managed to take over as the Governor General of Pakistan on 17 April, 1951. He is the one who earned the dubious distinction of, dissolving the Constituent Assembly, sacking Prime Minister Nazim-ud-Din and taking over the reins of the country on 17

April, 1953 by subverting the Constitution, he had sworn to uphold.

His action was challenged in the Sindh High Court, Which ruled against him. However, in the split judgement announced by Chief Justice Munir, the Supreme Court overturned the High Court judgement and validated the governor general's extra-constitutional action by invoking the maxim: "That which is otherwise not lawful is made lawful by necessity." The "friendly" judiciary was to rely on this "Doctrine of Necessity" to legitimise subsequent coups in Pakistan.

The country had to wait till Nov. 3, 2007 when a 14 - Judges bench of Pakistan Supreme Court presided over by Hon'ble Chief Justice Mr. Iftikhar Choudhary declared the emergency promulgated by President Mushaaraf and the consequent dismissal of judges as unconstitutional. So were the Provisional Constitutional Order (PCO), the Emergency Law and appointments of judges made under it. The Court further held that General Musharraf in his dual capacity as the Army Chief and the President had subverted the Constitution which amounted to treason under article 6 of 1973 Constitution of Pakistan, an offence punishable with death penalty, or life imprisonment. The pernicious Doctrine of Necessity was thus buried hopefully beyond resurrection.

To resume our survey, Governor General Malik Ghulam Mohammad proceeded on leave of absence in August, 1955 on account of deteriorating health condition. Interior minister Iskander Mirza, a civil servant of Military background, was installed as the acting Governor General. Mirza found the position cosy, and decided to stay on. He became the first President of Pakistan under the 1956 Constitution which declared Pakistan a Republic.

In October 1958, President Iskander Mirza usurped power by dissolving the Constituent Assembly and dismissing the government of Prime Minister Feroz Khan Noon. Army commander-in-chief Gen. Ayub Khan was named the Chief martial law administrator confirming a tie up between Mirza and the Pak army. President Eisenhower of the USA, who had been sounded in advance, formally endorsed the coup through a letter addressed to the Pakistan President. Thirteen days later, Mirza himself was deposed by Ayub Khan who appointed himself as the President. Thus commenced the era of Military dictators in the Republic of Pakistan.

The assassination of Liaquat Ali Khan plunged an unstable and less than efficiently administered Pakistan into fathomless abyss of corruption and administrative chaos. The extent of instability can be gauged from the fact that seven Prime Ministers took the oath of office and departed unceremoniously between 1951 and 1958. During this period Army, a competent, well knit, disciplined, patriotic institution led by highly professional commanders was the only stabilising component of Pakistan power structure. They also had the unique distinction of enjoying popular reverence.

Despite these assets and their serious worry about what was happening, the army leadership chose to stay apolitical and refrained from meddling in politics. There is also a perception that but for Iskander Mirza's act of involving army in civilian government by appointing Commander-in-chief Gen. Ayub Khan as Defence Minister in Ali Md. Bogra's cabinet while he retained the command of the Pakistan Army and taking him on board the conspiracy to stage the 1958 coup, the history of Pakistan may have been different. It is, however, a fact of history that once the Army dictators tasted power, they clung to it with all the tenacity they could muster. Ironically, Gen. Yaya Khan, the "drunkard and debauched" was the only exception. He did not stage a coup but succeeded a totally discredited Ayub Khan. And when his time came to go, he quietly quit in favour of Z.A. Bhutto, the leader of the majority party who was also appointed the Civilian Martial Law Administrator. Gen. Yaya's crowning achievement was to have held the only fair and free election in the history of Pakistan.

The other two Military rulers fallowed the conspiracy, treachery, lies and subversion of Constitution route. Zia promised to hold "free and fair" elections in October 1977 and assured that "Soon after the polls, power will be transferred to the elected representatives of the people". He would have perhaps stayed on and on but for the mysterious air crash on 17 August, 1988 which cut his life span short. Musharraf on the other hand was ousted following an adverse judicial judgement, a huge public outcry and elections to the National Assembly but not before he had undermined the popularity, prestige, credibility and very reputation of the Pakistan Army. This was summed up by a political commentator in Dawn (The widening gulf) in following words:

"I have never seen the level of anger towards the military and the intelligence that is presently evident in the media and on the Internet. Normally, this is Pakistan's holiest of sacred cows."

For obvious reasons, the focus remained on the developments leading to unconstitutional takeover and conduct of affairs of the country by Army Rulers. But for the exercise to be comprehensible and credible it was necessary to trace and expose the bureaucratic/civilian players who were the first to usurp power in violation of the Constitution of the country.

The Bhutto regime intervened between two military dictatorships. It was both the cause and consequence of initiatives by Military dictators, and indexed their motivations and mindset. An insight into the interplay of stakeholders and consequent train of events was therefore absolutely necessary for any just comprehension of the period Pakistan remained under Army dictatorship.

Indian concerns with political, strategic, economic, and diplomatic developments in Pakistan were natural, necessary and abiding. Our neighbours' lust for territory, irrational obsession with fears of Indian hegemony and animosity syndrome have plagued Indo-Pak relations from day one.

Militarisation of its polity has had the effect of spawning three full scale wars and the mini Kargil war. It was also at the root of the more than two decades old cross-border terrorism which spilled over from Jammu and Kashmir to the length and breadth of the country. Horrible crimes like 26/11 Mumbai carnage, attack on Parliament and recent intrusion by Pakistan army and Lashkar goons in Poonch sector brutally murdering two Indian soldiers, chopping off and decamping with the head of one of the them can be directly attributed to this mindset.

The anger and outrage against the horrendous crime and grave provocation by the Pakistan army was compounded by Pakistan establishment resort to blanket denial. Respecting the strong national sentiment the Government of India, after some initial hesitation did take a tough position. The chief of Army Staff declared that Indian army will appropriately respond "at the time and place of its choosing" and added that he "expected his field commanders to respond offensively and aggressively" to any provocation. The Prime Minister categorically stated that "there can not be business as usual" in face of this barbarous and shameful act of Pakistan Army.

The response from the India state was hugely influenced by the unrelenting public pressure mainly triggered by the Media campaign and regular exposures. This underlines the need and urgency of people of India gaining an informed, objective, credible and comprehensive perspective about Pakistan, the institutors that make it tick and the scourge of non-state actors" wedded to political Islam-strategic assets of Pakistan establishment.

"Pakistan under Army rule"attempts to comprehensively and objectively study, survey, evaluate and interpret factors and events that went into making Pakistan vulnerable to Army "take-over." It lends perspective to events and highlights the role of personalities preceding, and during the fateful days exposing conspiracies and illuminating many grey and dark areas. It is my hope and expectation that readers, will find its study useful and helpful, may be in a small way in crafting an informed and realistic Pakistan perspective enabling them to influence the national policies towards our belligerent and crafty neighbour.

(M.M. Khajooria)

'Sahil'

Gandhi Nagar, Jammu
06 August, 2013

PART-I

1

A Home Land for Muslims of British India

The 1947 partition of the British India was a terribly messy and bloody operation. The birth of the state of Pakistan was preceded and accompanied by a human tragedy of gargantuan proportions, unprecedented in the history of mankind. It was indeed baffling that neither the British who facilitated the partition, nor Jinnah and Muslim League which spearheaded the demand for Pakistan on the basis of pernicious "Two Nations Theory" anticipated the logical outcome of their enterprise. Migration of ten lakh of people from either sides of the divide and unprecedented communal riots were undoubtedly consequences of the strategically crafted "Direct Action" call by the Muslim League. The edifice of the separate Home land for the Muslims of British India was built on huge piles of dead bodies of innocent victims of communal frenzy soaked in rivers of blood.

From day one of its existence, Pakistan had problems in three critical areas—political talent, bureaucracy and defence services. The Muslim League suffered from a famine of political talent and organisational competence in provinces which constituted Pakistan, as it enjoyed little support in these parts. These provinces were therefore poorly represented in the higher echelons of Muslim league leadership as well as in legislatures.

There was a huge gap between the demand and supply of experienced and competent local Muslim League leaders capable of managing the affairs of the State and manning the central and provincial governments. The fact that both the first Governor General, Mohd. Ali Jinnah and the first Prime Minister Nawabzada Liaquat Ali Khan were migrants and, despite his precarious health condition Mohd. Ali Jinnah, the Governor General was compelled to simultaneously saddle himself with the onerous responsibility of presiding over the Constituent Assembly illustrates the point tellingly.

At the time of the partition, Officers serving the British Indian government were granted the option to choose either of the two Dominions for future service. As India decided to remain a secular entity wedded to parliamentary democracy, large number of senior and experienced Muslim officers belonging to provinces that formed part of the Indian Dominion there fore preferred to stay on and resist the temptation to venture into a distant and "alien" Home land for Muslims of the sub-continent. Pakistan's share from the civil services pool was therefore far from flattering.

Deficient in quality instruments of governance, Pakistan soon fell prey to maladministration and rampant corruption. Unencumbered by any worthwhile supervision, Field officers made hay at the cost of the common man. Many senior bureaucrats felt more comfortable in engaging in palace intrigues and playing dirty politics than perform the mundane task of administering the country. The people of Pakistan naturally held them responsible for the rot that had set in the administration and for good reasons. An atrociously corrupt and unjust governance apparatus soon forfeited the public trust.

- The Pakistan Army was created on 30 June, 1947 with the division of the British Indian Army. Even though Pakistan's share of officers was inadequate, those who came to the share of Pakistan had combat experience and were well groomed by the experienced British Officers. As the army regiments were ethnically packaged even officers not hailing from the territory that formed Pakistan were culturally and psychologically integrated. An officer of the Punjab regiment was a Punjabi, his place of origin not withstanding. He spoke the language, enjoyed the Punjabi food, dressed as a Punjabi and scrupulously observed all their customs. The men and Viceroy commissioned officers (as the JCOs were then known) accepted them as such without any reservation. And veteran junior commissioned officers, non-commissioned officers and trained, disciplined and motivated *jawans* constituted the real strength of Pakistan army. In fact, Pakistan Army was known as company commanders army. Moreover, the Pakistan Army had done a good job during the chaotic period of migration thereby earning respect and gratitude of the people. It enjoyed good public image and was perceived as dependable defender of the *MUMALKAT_I_KHUDA DAD* (The God given country).

- The migrant political leaders and bureaucrats, on the other hand, were treated and behaved like uprooted aliens. They rated themselves as culturally sophisticated and superior and carried a hallow of martyrdom convinced that their sacrifices had made the dream of Pakistan come true. Enjoying superior status, the bureaucrats did not consider it necessary to woe the locals or try to integrate with the civil society. The position of migrant legislatures and other political leaders was even more precarious. Their constituencies were left behind, support bases disintegrated and cadres dispersed. Societies in provinces forming Pakistan were feudal, or tribal in character. Areas of influence and commitment of followers and supporters were almost iron clad. The local leaders were civil in behaviour but unwilling to defer to 'Hindustani *Maharajas*' in matters of leadership. Fundamentally, there was conflict between ethnicity and religion. And as always ethnicity prevailed. The Punjabis, Pathans, Sindhis and Baloachs were quite sympathetic towards Hindustani Muslim migrants, willing to help in any manner they could but most certainly not willing to be ruled by them. This dichotomy was to significantly colour the future course of history of Pakistan.

2

An Era of Instability

The fast deteriorating health of Mohd. Ali Jinnah was perhaps the most well guarded state secret of Pakistan. The announcement of his "Sudden" demise on 11 September, 1948, therefore, shocked the surprised nation beyond measure. A wave of pessimism appeared to be taking hold of the nation. Who will fill the void? The question rang out loud and clear throughout the country. Prime Minister Liaquat Ali Khan, however, rose to the occasion and managed to work out a consensus upon the name of Sir Khwaja Nazimuddin to be the second Governor General of Pakistan.

A Bengali Muslim League leader of eminence and a cabinet minister, Kh. Nazimuddin had remained Education Minister in the united Bengal government from 1929 to 1934 and Member of the viceroy's Executive Council from 1934 to 1937. Born in the family of Nawabs of Dhaka, a great-grandson of the last Nawab of Bengal Mir Jafar, and an aristocrat by nature, he became a darling of the bureaucracy whose expertise in sycophancy and manipulation was the talk of the town.

The fledgling state was engaged in grappling with massive and mounting problems of governance deficit and political instability when another tragedy struck. Prime Minister Liaquat Ali Khan was assassinated on 17 October, 1951. The loss of the *Quid-i-Azam* Mohd. Ali Jinnah, the creator of

Pakistan and his trusted and capable second-in-command, Prime Minister Liaqat Ali Khan in such a short span of time that, too, in the very infancy of Pakistan immeasurably enhanced fears of instability and insecurity. At that point of time, public perceived that Pakistan Army alone had the credentials and capability to preserve the unity and integrity of the country. But the army leadership held back. This faith and trust that the Pakistan Army enjoyed in the country was, however, to influence the course of event in not too distant future.

Malik Ghulam Mohammad

Malik Ghulam Mohd., the Finance Minister emerged as the consensus candidate for Prime ministership. An ambitious manipulator he had actually set his eyes on the top slot where in the real power resided the office of the Governor General. Ghulam Mohd. managed to win over a bunch of bureaucrats close to Nawab Nazimuddin and tasked them to persuade him to vacate Governor Generalship for Ghulam Mohd. and assume the charge of Prime minister instead. They were successful in convincing Nazimuddin that the arrangement would be good for him as well as beneficial for the country as under the Constitution in the making real power would soon vest in the Prime Minister. Consequently Nazimuddin gave his concurrence for being appointed as the Prime Minister. Malik Ghulam Mohd. eased into the seat of real power as the Governor General on 17 October, 1951. The era of palace intrigues and subversion of Constitution had dawned.

It took Ghulam Mohd. less than two years, on 17 April, 1953 to be precise, to summarily sack Prime Minister Nazimuddin in exercise of extra-constitutional emergency powers, dissolve the Constituent Assembly and appoint a new Council of Ministers on the ground that the Constituent Assembly no longer represented the people.

Maulvi Tamiz-ud-din, the president of constituent assembly challenged Governor General's action in the Sindh High Court, which ruled in his favour. However, Ghulam Muhammad won the case in the Supreme Court, though the verdict was split. In what would prove to be a landmark judgement delivered by Chief Justice Munir, the governor general's 1954 extra-constitutional sack order was validated using the maxim: "That which is otherwise not lawful is made lawful by necessity." Thus the "Doctrine of Necessity" was invoked for the first time to legalise an extra-constitutional action. This marked the beginning of what came to be known as "viceregal" politics enabling the military and civil bureaucracy to usurp power and exercise overriding influence over society and the government.

Major General Iskander Mirza

In 1955 Ghulam Muhammad proceeded on leave of absence on account of deteriorating health condition. Interior minister Iskander Mirza, took over as acting Governor General. He liked the job and decided to stay on and assumed the office of the President of Pakistan on March, 1958 under the new Constitution.

The country was going through a prolonged spell of instability. It witnessed the spectacle of seven different Prime ministers entering and leaving the exalted office between 1951 to 1957. Moreover, he did not see much of future for his Republican party in the forthcoming election under the 1956 Constitution. To him the political climate appeared to be favourable for assuming absolute power provided he was able to muster the support of General Ayub Khan, the chief of the Army Staff. General Ayub Khan, a serving Commander-in-Chief, was inducted into Muhammad Ali Bogra's Federal Cabinet and allotted the portfolio of Defence — thereby directly involving the military in politics of the country for the first time. As Commander-in-Chief and Defence Minister, Ayub Khan played a key role in negotiations concerning Pakistan's entry into United States' sponsored military alliances, CENTO and SEATO. Having "won over" General Ayub Khan to his plan, Mirza summoned chiefs of the air force and the navy to the President House in the early evening of October 7, 1958 and informed them of what the two of them planned to do that evening. The first coup in the history of Pakistan was thus executed smoothly without shedding a drop of blood. The president imposed martial law and appointed General Ayub Khan as the chief Martial Law Administrator.

In a move of far reaching significance, Iskandar Mirza took the US government in confidence about the planned coup couple of days before the event through US ambassador to Pakistan. Within four days of the military take-over President Eisenhower, himself an ex-General, sent a letter to Iskandar Mirza endorsing the coup.

As subsequent developments would reveal, Iskander Mirza and Ayub Khan were only united on the resolve to stem the rot in politico-administrative system, otherwise each had his own perception and agenda."

"Its (Isikander Mirza's plan) essential elements" wrote columnist Col. (Retd) G H Niaz in his piece titled Pakistan Army (The Misplaced Sojourn) "were abrogation of the Constitution, imposition of martial law by using General Ayub Khan and the Army and after dust settled, scheme was to kick out General Ayub Khan and appoint a docile and pliable Commander-in-Chief in his place and thus rule the country undisturbed. With the Army Chief behind him and Americans all out to help him with economic and other aid, he thought he would be the king of Pakistan for life." "Unfortunately for him things did not quite work out according to his plan. Martial Law was declared on 8th October, 1958 with Isikander Mirza as President but the Army under the leadership of General Ayub Khan took over the government from him on 27th October" he concluded.

Apparently, Iskander Mirza had grossly miscalculated. It was axiomatic that in any contest for power, the one in command of army will always prevail over the person occupying a distant titular position, whatever its civilian status. In this particular case, Mirza had even lost the moral authority by abrogating the very Constitution from which his powers flowed. In any case, Ayub Khan and the army command was determined to turn out the "inefficient and rascally" politicians—a task easily accomplished. That, too, without bloodshed.

3

Army Chief in the Driving Seat

Field Marshal Ayub Khan

Ayub Khan justified his assumption of power by citing the nation's need for stability which made it incumbent upon the army, the only organised, disciplined and manifestly patriotic organisation to play a central role in the affairs of the state.

On the assumption of presidency by General Ayub Khan, the prime minister's cabinet took oath as the presidential cabinet. In a singularly courageous move Ayub Khan gave up the post of Chief of Pakistan Army and appointed General Muhammad Musa as its commander-in-chief.

The vigour and enthusiasm with which the bloodless and smooth October 27, 1958, military coup was welcomed unequivocally established popular rejection of the elitist politico-bureaucratic combine, their self-serving policies, palace intrigues and abhorrent corrupt practices. The Pakistan army on the other hand was seen as the savior, by and large free from the taint of corruption which could be trusted to administer the country with a sense of responsibility, sensitiveness and commitment to the larger cause of welfare of the citizens of Pakistan. Hopes of a clean, fair and just administration ran high. The rank and file of the Pakistan Army were also happy to be seen as harbingers of order and prosperity for their beloved motherland.

The coup heralded the ascendancy of the military and eclipse of "the discredited" political elite who were driven to the margins of the political system.

Precisely one year after military takeover on October 27, 1959, the exalted rank of Field Marshal was conferred on General Ayub Khan by the presidential cabinet. On the same day, Ayub Khan unveiled his vision of "democratic structures" at the grass root level called "Basic Democracies". This was the first public indicator of his philosophy of governance in which army held the real power camouflaged by a civilian façade. He made out the case that Western form of democracy did not gel with the genius of people of Pakistan. A guided and limited democracy functioning under his benevolent military dispensation was the only practical, viable and desirable system of governance suited to Pakistan. This strategy of projecting civilian façade for an essentially Military controlled government became the sacred Mantra for the future military dictators like Zia-ul-Haq and Parvez Musharraf.

"Perhaps the single biggest reason people remember Ayub's era fondly is because it was the time when Pakistan first acquired a relatively sizable manufacturing base. And indeed, manufacturing growth in Pakistan during his time was 8. 51 per cent, far outpacing any other time in Pakistani history. It was the time when Pakistan first got an automobile industry, a cement industry and few other heavy manufacturing industries," wrote Farooq Trimizi in his analytical piece captioned "How golden was Ayub Khan's era?" (May 14, 2012-Express Tribune). "But is that enough to remember it with misty-eyed fondness?" he questions and answers himself. "He (Ayub Khan) laid rotten foundations to Pakistan's economy that achieved growth, but have made us a highly noncompetitive economy dominated by rent-seeking industrial lobbies, all of whom want government subsidies but cry bloody murder when asked to pay taxes. Indeed, if the economy was really doing so well during Ayub

Khan's era, why was tax collection so low (averaging less than 10 per cent of GDP"? He demanded, "The decade of development" under Ayub witnessed a phenomenal growth of income inequality, an issue that inspired his own Planning Commission chairman, Dr. Mehboob-ul-Haq, to deliver his famous 1969 "22 families" speech.

Ayub Khan persisted with his predecessors' policy of alliances with the West. Pakistan joining CENTO allowed Anglo-American's access to facilities inside Pakistan, most notably the use for launching U-2 intelligence flights over the Soviet Union. He also strengthened ties with neighbouring China. The reign of Ayub Khan also contributed to increasing political tensions in East Pakistan. The discrimination against East Pakistan went to the extent that tariffs were levied on products arriving from East Pakistan to West Pakistan but products going to the Eastern wing from Western wing were exempt from such tariffs. The foundation of the parting of ways between Eastern and Western wings of Pakistan were demonstratively laid during his tenure.

By 1960, Ayub Khan was running out of tricks. The farce of a "Guided" referendum on the basis as a kind of electoral college, comprising around 80,000 "elected village councilmen" on a yes, or no vote to the question: "Have you confidence in the President, Field Marshal Mohammed Ayub Khan?" won him 95.6 per cent of the votes but, exposed the hollowness of his much trotted popularity. Whatever was left of his public acceptability was gravely damaged by the massively rigged Presidential poll of 1965 in which he defeated Fatima Jinnah, the sister and life long companion of *Baba-I-Quam*, Mohd Ali Jinnah. The disastrous war with India the same year that concluded with the Tashkent Agreement, proved the proverbial last straw. In addition policies of concentrating political power in his own hands, exercising control over the media and imposing state of emergency in the country, were also responsible for his downfall. Adding insult to injury, Ayub Khan decided to celebrate the decade of his rule in 1968 and made exaggerated claims about the development in the country.

From 1967 onwards public resentment against Ayub Khan and his government mounted dramatically. Zulfiqar Ali Bhutto, deserted him and launched his own party, the Pakistan People's Party, with the aim to remove him from power. The Awami League under Sheikh Mujib-ur-Rahman dubbed him as pro West Pakistan and alleged that the Bengali's were denied their rights. The other political parties formed an alliance, the Democratic Action Committee, with a one-point agenda, removal of Ayub Khan's government.

By the end of 1968, a powerful *"Ayub Hatao"* movement was launched in which the urban-middle class, students, teachers, lawyers, doctors, and engineers participated in large numbers. The Joint Labour Council called for a general strike. Demonstrations and agitation were held across the country. Law and order broke down. Ayub was left with no other option but to leave. On March 25, 1969, Field Mashal Ayub Khan stepped down from the presidency and handed over the power to the Commander-in-Chief of Pakistan Army, General Muhammad Yahya Khan.

4

General Yahya Khan Takes Turn

Immediately after taking over from Ayub Khan, General Yahya Khan declared martial law for the second time in the history of Pakistan on March 25, 1969, and assumed the title of Chief Martial Law Administrator. The Constitution was terminated and National and Provincial Assemblies dissolved. On March 31, he also became President of the Islamic Republic of Pakistan.

Unlike his predecessors, Yahya Khan was not interested in prolonging his rule. He had inherited a grand mess. He also seemed to recognise that the March 1969 change over was not welcome to the nation because they suffered under failed army dispensations for 11 long years and had no appetite for any more of the same.

To gauge the mood of the political class across the board, he held talks with a number of politicians included Mumtaz Daultana, Maulana Maudoodi, Sardar Shaukat Hayat, Nawabzada Nasrullah Khan, Nurul Amin, Hamidul Haq Chaudhry, Shaikh Mujibur Rahman, in Lahore and Dhaka. This exercise resulted in his resolve to hold General elections at the earliest.

The Legal Framework Order was issued on March 29, 1970 through an Ordinance, laying down the format according to which the forthcoming elections were to be held. Yahya Khan deserved the credit for holding in December 1970 the first and perhaps the only fair general elections in the history of Pakistan.

The results were on predictable lines. Sheikh Mujib-ur-Rahman's Awami League, swept the polls in East Pakistan capturing 160 out of 162 seats. The Awami League, however, drew a blank in west Pakistan. In West Pakistan, Zulfiqar Ali Bhutto's Pakistan People's Party emerged as the single largest party winning 81 National Assembly seats from Punjab and Sindh. This split mandate created an untenable situation. The President as well as Bhutto were dead set against handing over the reins of government to Mujib-ur-Rehman, which was his right as leader of the dominant party in the National assembly. Nor was there any meeting ground between Bhutto and Mujib. They could not even agree on the date of convening the newly elected National Assembly session. The ball thus bounced back into the court of the president. This political crisis of huge and varied dimension demanded statesmanship, which certainly was not Yahya Khan's forte. In stead of persisting with mediation and working for conciliation, he went shamelessly partisan deploying army and paramilitary forces in East Pakistan to crush the Awami League agitation. The ethnic cleansing, mass murders of Bengali intellectuals, gang rapes and other acts of brutality gave rise to "Mukti Vahini" and led to war with India in the winter of 1971.

Yahya Khan, as President as well as the Commander-in-Chief of Pakistan Army, miserably failed to plan and persecute the war with professional élan. As a result Pakistan, suffered defeat. Lt. General Niazi leading the Pakistan Army in East Pakistan formally surrendered before Lt. General Jagjeet Singh of the Indian Army which took a record number of more than 90,000 Pakistan army officers and soldiers as war prisoners.

The dismemberment of the country, surrender of Pakistani forces and the fall of Dhaka made Yahya Khan the greatest villain in the country. He had to go. It was agreed that Zulfikar Ali Bhutto, the leader of the most popular party of the remaining part of Pakistan should relieve him. ZA Bhutto was, at that time in New York presenting Pakistan's case on the East Pakistan Crises before the United Nations Security Council. A Pakistan International Airlines aircraft was chartered to fly him home.

A War Inquiry Commission appointed in December 1971 was headed by Chief Justice Hamoodur Rahman. The commission held widespread atrocities, other abuses of power by Pakistani generals and a complete failure in civilian and martial-law leadership responsible for the loss of East Pakistan. The report dwellsed on a range of sins: killing of thousands of Bangladeshis—both civilians and "Bengali" soldiers—rape, smuggling, looting of banks in East Pakistan, drunkenness by officers, even an instance of a Brigadier "entertaining" women while his troops were being shelled by Indian troops. It recommended a string of court-martials and trials against top officers. Nothing ever happened. The army's role in splintering Pakistan after its greatest military debacle was largely ignored by successive Pakistani governments.

The commission was also reported to have gone into shocking details of President Yahya Khan's drunkenness and debauchery drawing out a detailed list of his favourite women, most prominent being "his close friend and domestic partner Akleem Akhtar, otherwise known as General Rani and a top class singer and actress enjoying tremendous popularity in Pakistan as well as India. 'General Rani' allegedly ran a vast high class callgirl network. Even during the war Yahya Khan would spend lot more time in drinking and womanising to the gross neglect of his daunting and onerous responsibilities as Head of the state and Commander-in-Chief of Pakistan Army. No wonder Pakistan suffered a humiliating defeat in the 1971 war and lost its Eastern wing which emerged as Bangladesh on the world map.

5

The Civilian Chief Martial Law Administrator

On return, Bhutto was sworn in as President and Chief Martial Law Administrator in the Aiwan-I-Sadar, at Rawalpindi on 20 December 1971—the first civilian to don the mantle of Chief Martial law administrator of a truncated Pakistan.

Bhutto assumed control of what remained of Pakistan at a time of great-national distress. The nation was smarting under the crushing and humiliating defeat suffered by the army they were led to believe was invincible. His first task, therefore, was to reach out to the people of Pakistan shake them out of despondency and assure them that with determination and united effort they could and would put Pakistan back on the track. A great orator, he was eminently cut out for the task. In his radio and television address he said:

"My dear countrymen, my dear friends, my dear students, labourers, peasants...those who fought for Pakistan...We are facing the worst crisis in our country's life, a deadly crisis. We have to pick up the pieces, very small pieces, but we will make a new Pakistan, a prosperous and progressive Pakistan, a Pakistan free of exploitation, a Pakistan envisaged by the Quaid-e-Azam." This done, he got down to business in great earnest.

During his tenure as president and the Prime minister of Pakistan, Bhutto took certain initiatives, formulated policies and set the country on a course, the succeeding governments of Pakistan continue to tread. The most important measures taken during his stewardship of Pakistan were:

(1) Bhutto pushed through the national assembly the Constitution proclaiming Pakistan as the "Islamic Republic" (Concession to sentiments) but with a parliamentary form of government. It became effective from 10 August, 1973. President Bhutto witched positions with Fazal Ilahi Chaudhry, assuming the office of prime minister, the centre of real power under the 1973 constitution.

(2) By July 1972, Bhutto had managed to recover 93,000 prisoners of war and 5,000 square miles of Indian-held territory under the Simla Agreement. The Indian gesture of accommodation, however, failed to soften his belligerence towards the bigger neighbour.

(3) He tilted the foreign policy of the country in a non-aligned direction and stoutly persisted with the "befriend China" policy to build a powerful counter poise against India He significantly enlarged the sphere of Sino-Pak economic and defence co-operation.

(4) Bhutto was called father of Pakistan nuclear programme. He authorised a comprehensive atomic power development programme and inaugurated the first Pakistani atomic reactor, at Karachi built in collaboration with Canada.

(5) On 2 January 1972, he announced the nationalisation of all major industries, including iron and steel, heavy engineering, heavy electrical, petrochemical, cement and public utilities. A new labour policy was announced increasing workers rights and the power of trade unions. Although he came from a feudal background himself, Bhutto announced reforms limiting land ownership and a government take-over of over a million acres (4,000 km) to distribute to landless peasants. More than 2,000 civil servants were dismissed on charges of corruption.

(6) In pursuance of his promise to the nation to build a professional and well-trained Defence machine he undertook re-organisation of the Defence services. Bhutto disbanded the rank of Commander-in-Chief in the Pakistan Armed Forces and re-organised country's intelligence services. As part of this vision, all three service chiefs, of Air Force, Navy and Army were appointed 4-star Generals. The post of Joint Chiefs of Staff Committee was created and senior 4-star General, General Muhammad Sheriff appointed as its first chairman.

The pronounced tilt towards China in foreign policy and people friendly socialist measures alarmed the United Sates government. The US wanted Bhutto out as early as possible.

He successfully negotiated and reached an understanding with opposition leaders, Abdul Wali Khan and Mufti Mahmud. The state of emergency was lifted enabling the Opposition to form governments in those provinces.

Bhutto painstakingly and competently created a vast party network of a cadre-based and left oriented political machine named Pakistan People's Party. Having gone through a spell of long struggle, suffered repression and persecution, the workers were hardened fighters, loyal to Bhutto and committed to the causes, the party espoused. Lot of blood and sweat had gone into building and sustaining the spirit of the Pakistan People's Party.

These and other people friendly measures should have and did indeed make him the darling of the people of Pakistan, an iconic figure. These assets were, however, squandered away.

Bhutto's tenure as Prime Minster was assessed by U.S. Embassy, Pakistan, as fallows;

"During Bhutto's five years in Pakistan's helm, Bhutto had retained an emotional hold on the poor masses who had voted for him overwhelmingly in 1970s general elections. At the same time, however, Bhutto had many enemies. The [socialist economics] and nationalisation of major private industries during his first two years in office had badly upset the Business circles...An ill-considered decision to take over the wheat-milling, rice-husking, sugar mills, and cotton, industries in July of 1976 had angered the small business owners and traders. Both leftists—socialists and communists, intellectuals, students, and trade unionists—felt betrayed by Bhutto's shift to centre right wing conservative economic policies and by his growing collaboration with powerful feudal lords, Pakistan's traditional power brokers. After 1976, Bhutto's aggressive authoritarian personal style and often high-handed way of dealing with political rivals, dissidents, and opponents had also alienated many...."

Arrogant by nature, self opinionated to the point of grievous fault and of ever explosive short temper, it did not take much time for the unbridled power and public adulation to go to his head. He began to behave like a tyrant and a despot intolerant of any dissent thereby of losing friends and making fresh enemies. The party leaders did not receive the attention and courtesy they were accustomed to and the cadres felt left out and ignored by the bureaucracy. He hurt the pride of Pushtoon and Baloch nationalist leaders by not extending to them the basic courtesies. Undue and even crude interference in provincial affairs further widened the gulf. With leadership estranged and pride hurt the demand for independence from Pakistan peaked. Instead of inviting them to negotiate and find a way out for mutual cooperation and reconciliation, he ordered extensive military operations in these provinces. Nodoubt, the movements were brutally crushed but the seeds of long term hostilities were sown, which have since majored into ever intensifying insurgency.

Bhutto had to pay a very heavy price for his camel size ego, strong personal preferences, a closed mindset and the mistaken belief that he alone was right always and every time. He promoted General Zia-ul Haq as Chief of Pakistan Army over the heads of four seniors on the hasty and unsubstantiated assumption that he was, apolitical and submissive. Even other wise, these attributes could hardly qualify anyone to be installed as chief of an army like Pakistan army obsessed with "Indian evil designs to break it up"and perennially plagued by numerous internal conflicts and major regional and political problems. Bhutto refused to listen to words of caution sounded by some of his colleagues. He saw, he felt and he believed, Zia was the man for the exalted and crucial position. Unlike other politicians Bhutto enjoyed a good measure of respect and support in the Pakistan army. He, however, omitted to nurse this vital constituency.

On 3 July, 1977, then-Major-General KM Arif secretly met Bhutto and, revealed the planning of coup…taking place in the General Combatant Headquarters (GHQ). At this secret meeting, General Arif stressed Bhutto to "rush the negotiation with the PNA, before it is too late" (Haqani Hussain. Between Military and Mosque").

Bhutto rejected the information out of hand. His faith in a scheming and disloyal Zia-ul Haq was so strong that he dismissed General Arif. Understandably, other loyalists chose to stay quiet and remain neutral.

The very same General Zia meticulously planned the coup against him over a period of time which was covertly endorsed by the United States, under the administration of U.S. President Jimmy Carter. The CIA significantly contributed in spreading discontent and opposition against Bhutto and his government.

The 1977 election which "Bhutto's Pakistan People's Party won overwhelmingly" were believed to be massively rigged. Moreover, the entire alienated political class had unitedly raised the banner of revolt. Thousands of people took to streets. Unaware of the extent of the mass upsurge, or unmindful of the consequences of further precipitation, Bhutto ordered the arrest of opposition leaders, but soon backed down in face of rising protests and violence. Negotiators were started with opposition parties to hammer out a solution. But the "Mullah in Khaki" was watching. Sensing the mood of reconciliations

General Zia struck around midnight on July 4, 1977. He ordered the commander 111 Brigade Rawalpindi to encircle all major federal and provincial government buildings, police stations, and the National Assembly building. Orders were also issued to the police to take into custody Prime Minster Bhutto, his ministers, and leaders of both the Pakistan People's Party and the Pakistan National Alliance. In a nationally televised address, General Zia announced the suspension of Constitution and dissolution of the National Assembly and all provincial assemblies.

Bhutto was released on July 29, but re-arrested on September 3 to stand trial on charges of corruption and for the conspiracy to murder an opposition politician. The massive turn out at the Multan rally addressed by Bhutoo had frightened the regime.

On March 18, 1978, Zulfikar Ali Bhutto was sentenced to death for the murder of Nawab Muhammad Ahmad Khan Kasuri, the father of Ahmed Raza Kasuri. The entire process of investigation, prosecution and trial was vitiated under pressure from Zia-ul-Haq. The appeal to the Supreme Court was similarly influenced. Despite the appeals from 55 Heads of states, Zia persisted. Bhutto was hanged on 4 April, 1979, a hanging universally condemned as a "judicial murder".

ZA Bhutto ruled Pakistan for around six tumultuous years. His "Judicial murder" at the behest of his own protégé General Zia-ul Haq was a sad chapter in Pakistans' political history. His party survived and was till recently heading the coalition government in Pakistan. Some of the reforms undertaken by him and policies formulated, notably, the foreign policy regarding China remained the sheet anchor of Sino-Pak relations. Similarly, the nuclear agenda unveiled by him had since fructified.

6

Zia-ul Haq: The Mullah in Khaki

Having overthrown his benefactor in a treacherous US backed coup and safely locked up Bhutto, the new Chief Martial Law Administrator, General Zia-ul Haq addressed a bewildered nation on 5th July, 1977 only to tell a monumental lie. In his televised speech he affirmed his faith in democracy, and said "I genuinely feel that the survival of this country lies in the democracy alone"; and declared, "I want to make it absolutely clear that neither I have any political ambitions, nor does the army want to be taken away from its profession of soldiering. My sole aim is to organise free and fair elections which would be held in October this year. Soon after the polls, power will be transferred to the elected representatives of the people. I give a solemn assurance that I will not dissipate my power and energies as CMLA on anything else. I will do my best to refrain from doing anything which is likely to restrict the power of judiciary." But he did exactly what he had undertaken not to do. The period of three months got extended for almost eleven long years. His uninterrupted rule was cut short only by divine intervention. Zia-ul Haq was killed in an aircraft explosion on 17th August, 1988.

General Zia lied to the British journalist Edward Behr of Newsweek, when he claimed, "I (Zia) am the only man who took this decision. And I did so on 1700 Hrs on 4th July, after hearing the press statements that talks and negotiations between Mr. Bhutto and the Opposition had broken down. Had an agreement been reached between them, I certainly would never had done it. In fact, "General Zia had been long planning to impose the Martial law and end of Bhutto's government since 1976, soon when he became chief of army staff. On multiple occasions, Zia deliberately concealed intelligence information and misguided Bhutto on various political matters" (Haqqani, Hussain, 2005, *Pakistan:Between Mosque and Military*).

Zia quietly arranged with the British SAS to organise staff and command courses to suit the timing of the coup. Army officers loyal to Bhutto were deputed for these courses and were required to remain on training, until the midnight of 4th July, 1979. Naval personnel loyal to Bhutto and his government were quietly removed from the Navy's active duty by Chief of Naval Staff Admiral Mohammad Shariff. There is no doubt that the British SAS and US CIA were on board the coup.

On the issue of the coup there was no unanimity amongst the three arms of defence services and senior army officers. Zia, therefore, pressured President Fazal Ilahi Chaudhry to post out the dissident incumbents and appoint his supporters, General Anwar Shamim as Chief of Air Staff; Admiral Caramatt Niazi as Chief of Naval Staff and Admiral Mohammad Shariff as Chairman of the Joint Chiefs of Staff. (Institute for Defence Studies and Analyses 1980, *Strategic analysis: The Naval dictatorship*, University of California). In this manner unanimous validation of 1979 coup by the Chiefs of Army, Navy, and Chairman Chiefs of Staff Committee was ensured. Known as the "Mullah in Khaki", Zia was a hard-boiled and deeply committed Pan-Islamic fundamentalist. Having built bridges with USA in the last days of Bhutto's regime and successfully removed him from power with the active support of Anglo-American bloc, he sensed the once in centuries dawned opportunity to further the Jehadi cause by brokering a deal between the short sighted United States and Islamist players of a long haul. Such a combine would achieve three objectives.

First, the eviction of Godless Soviets from Afghanistan. Second, Establishment of a Jehadi regime in Afghanistan. Third, Promotion of Jehad in Kashmir and acceleration of Khalistan movement in the Indian Punjab. He foresaw no difficulty either in obtaining control over the inflowing finances and military equipment or diverting portion of these to Kashmir and Punjab. Similarly, training facilities created for Mujahideen would be shared by Kashmiri militants. He was said to have been pleasantly surprised how easily the US establishment particularly the CIA happily fell in line.

After assuming the presidency in 1978 aided and assisted by Saudi Arabia, Zia was able to play a major role in helping the United States to secure the withdrawal of the soviets from the neighbouring Communist Afghanistan. His endorsement and support to the the Afghan Mujahideen against the Soviet occupation throughout the 1980s was fully recognised as a vital element that culminated in the USSR's defeat and withdrawal in 1989. This, however, led to Pakistan becoming home to millions of refugees loaded with heroin and weaponry in its already troubled frontier province. The so called "Mujahideen assets" acquired by Zia today threaten the very existence of Pakistan. China and the Islamic world remained in special focus in the foreign policy pursued by Pakistan under Zia.

Domestically, Zia passed broad-ranging legislations as part of state's Islamisation, acts criticised for fomenting religious intolerance. He vigorously pursued Pakistan's successful quest for atomic bombs. The space programme as spin-off of the atomic project, was restarted and industrialisation and corporatisation instituted. He was also credited with helping Pakistan's economy become among the fastest-growing in South Asia.

He denationalied and deregulated the industries nationalised by Bhutto and followed policies and programmes aimed at Islamisation of the state including the Pakistan Defence services with special focus on the Inter Services Intelligence (ISI). In this manner he set Pakistan on the path of "Islamic revival" infecting its state apparatus including the armed forces with fundamentalist virus. Most of current daunting problems of Pakistan can be traced to what Zia-ul Haq did, or did not do, whether in power, or before he successfully conspired to usurp power.

Army should have been his first love. It wasn't. "During this (ZIA's) period, wrote Columnist Col. (Retd) G H Niaz in his column "Fifty Years of the Pakistan Army-The Misplaced Sojourn", "the Army was taken away from its profession of soldiering. The Defence budget was indiscriminately spent on unrelated to the efficiency bearing projects. The indiscriminate promotion in the army specially in the higher ranks, made it the Army of Generals. To look after the welfare of senior officers quality houses were built for them at a nominal price, plots and land were distributed. Living accommodation for junior officers was given the lowest priority. With this state of affairs there was frustration in the junior ranks."

Zia-ul Haq was sought to be projected as a man of deep abiding Islamic faith bearing strong character. Of course, the history will judge him. It may, however, be pertinent to narrate the following two instances.

1. "......promoted as Lieutenant General he was appointed commander of the II Strike Corps at Multan in 1975. It was during this time that Zia invited Prime Minister Zulfikar Ali Bhutto as the Colonel-in-Chief of the Armoured Corps at Multan, using his tailor to stitch the Blue Patrols of his size. The next day, Bhutto was requested to climb a tank and engage a target, where the target was quite obviously hit. After the function, Zia met Bhutto, placed his hand on the Qur'an and said, "You are the saviour of Pakistan and we owe it to you to be totally loyal to you, Amin" (Abdul Hafiz, "Remembering Our Warriors: Babar The Great", Interview with Major-General Baber. *Defence Journal of Pakistan.)*

Bhutto was no hereditary king Emperor. He was the leader elected to manage the affairs of the state for five years. Where was the provocation to swear undying loyalty for the man. And that, too, sworn on the Holy Quran. Sycophancy of the worst order—wasn't it?

2. "In the summer of 1976, General Zia, who had superseded many senior lieutenant-generals, told Prime Minister Zulfikar Ali Bhutto": "Sir, I am so grateful to you for appointing me Chief of Army Staff. Not only myself, but my future generations will be eternally grateful to you for singling me out for such a great honour, and this is a favour which I can never forget." (The Herald, July 1990.) Of course, he tellingly expressed his gratitude-- by hanging his benefactor.

Another myth exploded related to his alleged spartan living style—a style befitting a pious practising Muslim. Here is a testimony that speaks volumes.

Khalid Hassan US-based correspondent wrote his piece, POSTCARD USA: The Pakistani flying carpet (*Daily Times*) as told by Capt. Javed Muzaffar, a retired PIA captain who lives in Houston"

"Once I had Begum Shafiqa Zia travelling on a routine DC-10 commercial flight from Islamabad to London. I was the operating captain. She was going for medical treatment. The traffic staff informed me that she was carrying 11 enormous suitcases (no extra baggage charges had been paid). Before take-off, I saw her sprawled on two first class seats. Gen. Zia had come to see her off and he waved to me from the tarmac. Another time, I had to ferry back a VVIP configured DC-10 from Islamabad to Karachi after Gen. Zia and his entourage had deplaned. I was astounded when I boarded the aircraft, wondering if it was the same DC-10 I knew so well. There were leather seats, plush carpets, a conference room, new curtains, a large curtained-off bedroom area, special cutlery and crockery and what have you. The leftover food my skeleton crew and I were served was out of this world. I just could not help thinking about the enormous cost of all that to our poor nation."

"It seems that the general public does not know that whenever a PIA aircraft is requisitioned for VVIP travel, it is luxuriously "refurbished", only to be reconfigured later for the plebeians who pay to fly. There are already 15 aircraft, including helicopters, in the Pakistani VVIP fleet. There is a Boeing 707, an almost new luxuriously fitted Boeing 737, a Falcon executive jet, a Cessna Citation and an Airbus 310 gifted by Qatar. On top of that, three new Lear-jets have been purchased recently at a cost of $60 million. I would ask readers to think about the astronomical cost of hangaring, maintaining, certifying, fuelling, crewing and catering involved here." Striking a comparison with democratic India, he wrote and concluded, "Take India. Once I was parked in an Airbus 300 at Bombay Airport when I saw an Indian Airline Airbus taxiing in. It was a normal passenger flight. The door opened and outwalked Prime Minister Mrs. Indira Gandhi. One man took her briefcase, another held an umbrella over her head and she got into a beat-up white Ambassador and drove away. Perhaps therein lies the difference between the two neighbours."

Zia-ul Haq lifted martial law and held non-partisan elections in 1985. He, however, assumed even more presidential powers via the Eighth Amendment of the Constitution. Muhammad Khan Junejo was appointed as the prime minister. Junejo was dismissed for the sins of signing the Geneva Convention and Ordering an inquiry into devastating fire in the Ojhrai Ammunition Depot—from which huge number of weapons and tons of ammunition were believed to have been syphoned off to the Mujahideen engaged in Kashmir front. Fresh elections were announced for November 1988.

A mysterious air crash near Bahawalpur on 17th August, 1988 killed General Zia-ul Haq along with several of his top generals, admirals, and the then-United States Ambassador to Pakistan, Arnold Lewis Raphel. A board of inquiry was set up to investigate the crash. The truth has not been revealed. But there was consensus that the explosion and the crash was as "inside job – a conspiracy." One version making rounds was that "the most probable cause of the crash was a criminal act of sabotage perpetrated in the aircraft. It also suggested that poisonous gases were released which incapacitated the passengers and crew, which would explain why no Mayday signal was given. "

In his book "*Pakistan, A Dream Went Sour*", Roedad Khan, who served as Secretary-General for the Internal Security testified:

"(Zia)...wanted to become an Amir, a ridiculous concept which died centuries ago. If he (Zia) had his way, (Zia) would have taken [Pakistan] back to the Middle Ages...[Zia] had no idea of law, or [Constitution], or the requirements of a [modern] governments" (Khan, Roedad 1997, *Pakistan – A Dream Gone Sour*, Oxford University Press, p. 263).

Zia's exit only proved an intermission in the ongoing drama, perhaps a prolonged one. After nearly eleven years of tottering, feuding and military dependent "democratically" elected Prime Ministers and Presidents, Pakistan once again lapsed into Army rule. General Parvez Musharraf, the chief of staff ousted Prime Minister Nawaz Sheriff, enjoying impressive majority in the National Assembly and installed himself in the seat of power once again in a bloodless coup.

7

Musharraf Takes Over

A Military Coup?

In 1999, journalist Christina Lamb noticed an interesting graffiti on a wall in Karachi which read, "We apologise for this temporary democratic interruption. Normal martial law will be resumed shortly." It proved prophetic. On 12th October, 1999, General Parvez Musharraf, Chief of Army Staff and Chairman of the Joint Chiefs of Staff Committee overthrew the democratically elected Prime Minister Nawaz Sharif in a bloodless "Coup'd etat" and became Pakistan's *de facto* head of government. Pakistan did indeed return to Normal Martial law. He was the fourth Army chief to have usurped executive control since Pakistan emerged on the map of the world as a nation-state.

According to columnist Kamran Shafi, "The track record of authoritarian regimes is abysmal. The first military ruler, who had the brilliance to gift to Pakistan a democracy "suited to the genius of the people", initiated a war that sowed the seeds of separatism in the eastern wing. The second ignominiously lost half the country, while the third was unaware of the loss of strategic Siachen, so consumed was he by his passion to make us all good Muslims" (Dawn 1/11/2010).

General Parvez Musharraf, the man who executed "the coup" against the government led by Nawaz Sherif had been hand-picked by him to head the Pakistan Army ignoring the established system and over the head of his seniors. Ironically, 'obedience' was his perceived sterling quality. Apparently, no lesson was learnt from the experience of Zulfikar Ali Bhutto who also had in the very same manner catapulted his favourite junior General Zia-ul-Haq to the position Chief of Army Staff. Zia-ul-Haq not only ousted his benefactor but also had him 'judicially hanged.' Nawaz Sharif was lodged in Adiala Jail, infamous for hosting Zulfikar Ali Bhutto's trial. His leading defence Counsel, Iqbal Raad, was shot dead in Karachi in mid-March (McCarthy, Rory, *Guardian News,* 2000-03-11). The signs were ominous. Fortunately the lady luck smiled on him in the form of intervention by the Royal Saudi House otherwise Nawaz Sherif may have traversed the same route.

The reverses suffered by Pakistan in May-July 1999 Kargil war spawned a fierce controversy. The Prime Minister held Musharraf solely responsible for the Kargil fiasco. Musharraf stoutly denied the allegation and asserted that the decision on "Kargil war" was actually made by prime minister Nawaz Sherif who backed out when the going got tough and buckled under United States pressure. Both have vigorously presented their versions-Sherif in his "Gaddar Kaun" (Who is the traitor) and Musharraf in his Memoir (In the Line of Fire). In between these two subjective projections, numerous shades favouring one, or other main actors floated into the public domain. But truth, as always had to be somewhere in the middle perhaps incorporating elements from both versions. During my study, I found the disclosures made by Lt. Gen. (Retd) Jamshaid Gulzar Kiyani posted in ISI at that point of time, to Dr. Sahid Msassod in the GEO TV programme ("*Merey Mutabik*/According to Me") on June 03, 2008, closest to the truth. During the TV conversation Kayani said, "According to his information Nawaz Sharif did not know anything about the Kargil episode. He was never thoroughly briefed on the same." Asked what was his plan he said he had briefed Nawaz Sharif and told him that it was a very sensitive issue and he could not unveil all the details to him. He was only apprised of the ongoing situation. Nawaz, time and again asked about the truth from senior officials including Sartaj Aziz who was the foreign minister. He also tried to persuade General Majid "to apprise him of 'what was going on' but to no avail".

As the fighting on the heights of Kargil escalated into full fledged military engagement, the involvement of elements of Pakistan army in the conflict became an open secret. There were no takers for the Public Relations exertions by Pakistan Army projecting the fighting in Kargil sector of Jammu & Kashmir as extension of struggle for freedom by Kashmiri Mujhideen. The Pakistan Prime Minister demanded a full briefing about the operations and involvement of Pakistan Army. Discussions accordingly took place on the highest level on 17 May during which according to General Gulzar Kiyani, "He (Nawaz Sherif) assured conditional support to General Musharraf that the government would back the operation when he successfully moved forward. If unfortunately the same failed, he would not be in a position to support him (Musharraf)". Kayani termed Nawaz's travel to the US as a bid to save the prestige of the Pakistan Army, the disaster in Kargil notwithstanding.

A PTI despatch dated Oct. 3, 2006 from Islamabad quoted Lt . Gen. Ali Kuli Khan as saying, "Kargil was flawed in terms of its conception, tactical planning and execution. It was an unprofessional decision by someone who has served in the Pakistan Army for 40 years. As the architect of Kargil he must answer critical questions for sacrificing so many soldiers, lives..." (Published in DNA, Tuesday, Oct. 3, 2006, Agency PTI, Islamabad).

The schism in the Pakistan Defence forces was so sharp that Chief of air staff Air chief marshal Pervez Mehdi, Musharraf's life-long friend refrained to participate, or authorise any air strike to support the elements of army operations in the Kargil region. Qureshi even warned the then Prime Minister Nawaz Sharif that any PAK Air Force intervention into disputed land of Indian Kashmir would be perceived as an all-out war. Both Chiefs of Pakistan Air Force and Navy publically disclosed that Musharraf had not taken them on board in either planning, or execution of the Kargil operation.

On the battle field the Indians had snatched the initiative, reoccupied the strategically critical heights and infiltrators were on the run. Worried about nuclearisation of the conflict, US President Clinton forcefully intervened and brought the hostilities to a halt thereby bailing out Pakistan from a certain ignominious defeat.

The approval rating of Musharraf Kargil misadventure was the lowest ever in an Indo-Pak confrontation. The people were sceptical. The media mostly critical. The strategic community found the operation professionally flawed. The cessation of hostilities and ejection of Pakistan army personnel and their proxies from Kargil predictably led to a public clamour for apportioning responsibility for the disaster. There was also an outcry to identify and punish those responsible for inflicting the national shame. The open blame game between the Prime Minister, Nawaz Sherif and Chief of the Army Staff, General Musharraf gave rise to rumours of an imminent military coup.

The defence establishment was having problems of their own. No consensus could be arrived at between the army generals, most importantly corps commanders. The chiefs of Air Force and Navy were against a coup. Musharraf and his co-conspirators were thus forced to discard the option of preemption and go in for some alternative plan of action. A course of action was settled, engineered and perfected in complete secrecy on the bases of credible intelligence about the action Nawaz Sherif would take against General Musharraf. Subsequent developments testified both to the accuracy of the intelligence inputs and the course adopted by the Prime Minister.

The situation was favourable for Nawaz Sherif only if he could muster the courage to act decisively against Gen.

Musharraf. The General was perceived by a significant sections of establishment, the Army, the Media and the civil society to be personally responsible for the Kargil fiasco. Enjoying huge majority in the national assembly and constitutionally empowered Nawaz Sherif was ideally placed to relieve General Musharraf from the command and order his court martial. This action would have been logical, fair, correct and legal drawing the support even from a good number of army generals, serving as well as retired. The concurrence for this course of action by the Air Force and Naval chiefs could be taken for granted. However, lacking guts and self confidence, Nawaz Sherif decided to take the "conspiracy route."

A chronic bad judge of human character, this time, Nawaz bet on a weak, non-charismatic and incompetent Zia-ud-Din Butt who though heading the all powerful ISI was clueless about what was cooking in the Pakistan Army GHQ. Musharraf and his associate generals, on the other hand, appeared to have been fully cognizant of plans of the prime minister and his cronies which were of critical help in crafting their own plan of action. They were ready with response–structured, quick and decisive. The subsequent development proved them right and they won a clear and clean victory.

In his Memoir, 'In the Line of Fire', Gen. Musharraf describes his sacking by Prime Minister Nawaz Sherif as the coup and army's 'response' as the counter coup. "I have no compunction about admitting that the army was caught unawares by the prime minister's sudden action of dismissing me and following it up virtually simultaneously with sudden and abrupt changes in the military high command" (page 109, In the Line of Fire). Sorry General, no go. This pretence of innocence would not work. His removal and court martial, or military takeover were the two options being hotly debated in social, political and military circles. Both were thus on the cards.

On the question of Musharraf determination to topple Nawaz Sherif post-Kargil defeat, we have the unbiased and credible version of Admiral Bokhari, the then Chief of Naval

Staff. He told the *Tribune* correspondent Muhammad Shahzad on 9th October, 2002 that now he was free to speak because the minimum term to stay quiet after leaving the navy job had been completed. "I resigned on October 5, 1999, a week before Musharraf coup of October 12 because I had come to know that he had decided to topple the Sharif government". Asked why in his view Gen. Musharraf wanted to topple Nawaz Sharif, Admiral Bokhari categorically stated. "He feared he would be court martialled for masterminding the Kargil (debacle). I rang him up and told him that I was resigning. I could have stayed for another five months. He asked me not to resign...I said 'no' and insisted that I wanted to resign and he agreed," the *Tribune* quoted the former navy chief as saying (*Daily Times*, 9th Oct, 2002).

The story that "the chief of the general staff, Lt. General Mohammad Aziz Khan and Lt. General Mehmood were playing tennis in an army club in Chaklala, heard the news (about Musharraf removal) and hurried back to Army headquarters" (page 102) In the Line of Fire) to launch what he calls the 'counter coup' also does not wash." According to General Musharraf, "the counter coup–for there can be no other word for it – began at five PM, when the news of my removal was announced on television, and it took only three and a half hours. It would be over by 8. 30 PM when Lieutenant General Mehmood Ahmed entered the prime minister's house and took Nawaz Sharif into custody." (p. 120). Does he seriously expect anyone to believe that a coup, or call it counter coup if you please, to overthrow a constitutionally established and democratically elected prime minister enjoying huge majority in the national assembly could even be conceived by two Lt. Generals so casually and non chalantly to put at the helm of their country a sacked Chief of Army Staff literally hanging in the mid air? Remember, their actions not only violated the oath of allegiance sacred for any man in uniform, but amounted to mutiny. No sir, the coup was well planned and meticulously executed. All bets had been hedged. Lt. General Zia-ud-Din had been upstaged, and the loyalty of his organisation subverted. Deserted by his own organisation, he did not have the faintest idea of what Musharraf and Co. were upto.

Nawaz Sherif's decision of 12th October, 1999 to sack General Musharraf was perhaps substantially influenced by the ease with he was able to obtain the resignation of General Jehangir Karamat, the predecessor in office of General Musharraf. The switch over to his side by the chief of the powerful ISI, Lt. General Zia-ud-Din Butt and his associates further boosted his confidence. The absence of Gen. Musharraf from the country away in Sri Lanka on official business, perhaps precipitated the decision. Nawaz Sherif replaced Musharraf as Chief of the Army Staff by Lt. Gen. Zia-ud-Din Butt, the ISI chief, who was elevated to the rank of the prime minister's decision to remove the Chief of the Army Staff would be meaningless without simultaneously shifting Musharraf team from sensitive assignments to be filled up by officers chosen by the incoming chief of army staff General.

Unfortunately for Nawaz Sherif, General Butt failed to display the qualities of leadership, verve and thrust demanded by the hugely challenging situation. To put it mildly, he was unable to seize the tantalising opportunity. The prime minister had bet very heavily on a very weak horse. Instead of taking over control, make quick and strident moves to assert his authority and defang Musharraf supporters, he appeared to be content with piggyback riding the prime minister. It is indeed ironical that the so-called master spy was ignorant of the subversion of his own agency. Contrast this with the speed and sharp focussed operational thrust with which the Musharraf group, on the other hand, struck and took the prime ministers and others into custody. The daring seizure of the Karachi airport enabling Gen. Musharraf to land set the final seal. His bursting on the scene live and kicking deterred other Musharraf haters and fence-sitters from making any counter move. However, in the final analysis, it was the intense loyalty and commitment to the Pakistan Army as a sacred institution and

"Sheild of the Islamic Republic" that restrained the anti-Musharraf groups from joining battle. No one was willing to earn the odium of having destroyed the institution of the army and ignite intra army conflict.

The 1999 Pakistani "coup d'état" was truly bloodless. The troops loyal to General Musharraf just moved into prime minister's house and put Nawaz Sherif under house arrest. No resistance was offered even by those guarding him and his residence. Musharraf became *de facto* Head of Government of Pakistan (assuming the title *Chief Executive* enjoying extensive powers). He immediately got down to the task of validating his takeover and firm up his grip over the vital institutions of the state.

On 14th October, 1999, just two days after the coup, he declared a state of emergency and issued a Provisional Constitutional Order. He also had the Oath of Judges Order, 2000 issued which required the judges to take a fresh oath of office swearing allegiance to military rule and pass no order against the military. Some judges refused to oblige and quit. Interestingly, Justice Iftikhar Choudhry who was to prove to be Musharraf's undoing was not amongst the conscientious ones. The constitutional validity of Musharraf assumption of power was challenged through court petitions. No one was surprised when the Supreme Court rejected the petitions and Pak Judiciary held military takeover constitutionally valid. "The most unfortunate aspect of the history of Pakistan", wrote Justice (Retd.) Rasheed A. Razv in his book *Judicial Crisis in Pakistan*, "that the judiciary was always kept under restrain by all successive governments." "It is very painful to note that the judiciary in Pakistan has extended authority to military rulers to legislate and even to amend the Constitution," he lamented.

For the Dictator, the picture at home was quite rosy. Benazir Bhutto was in self-exile. Nawaz Shrief safely tucked in Saudi Arabia as a guest of the Royal House. The political class at home was in utter disarray. The traditional fence-sitters and habitual *Aaya Ram Gaya Rams* were vying with each other to get into the favour of the man in *Awan-i-saddr*. Most importantly, dissenters within the army were "dealt with", or sidelined further tightening control over the armed forces.

All other levers of state power and vital state institutions were fully secured. Mullah-Military alliance was in tact. The ISI was in control of the Afghan front and relations with Taliban and Al-Queda at its best. The proxy war in Jammu & Kashmir was, by and large proceeding according to plans. Only the economy was at the verge of collapse largely due to economic sanctions imposed by United States and NATO countries after Pakistan acquired nuclear capability in 1998. The investor confidence was at an all-time low. Fortunately for him people were generally putting up with the hardships without much protest as the question of national honour was perceived to be involved. And then 9/11 happened. The worst tragedy in the history of United States ironically proved a military-economic bonanza for Musharraf's Pakistan and salvaged the state at the verge of being declared a "failed state."

Post–9/11, when General Musharraf jumped on the US driven anti-terrorist bandwagon and "partnered" the hunt for Osama Bin Laden, international sanctions were lifted. To secure the best advantage from the cosy relations with USA, Musharraf appointed Shaukat Aziz, a former Citibank executive, as finance minister. World powers weighed in for debt reschedule to reward Pakistan for participation in the "war on terrorism." This produced saving of hundreds of millions of dollars. New loans were also generously sanctioned. Consequently, foreign exchange reserves increased exceeding $16 billion in 2006.

Back to 9/11. After watching "Smoke from burning aircraft fuel and the dust and debris from the largest building in the world made the scene look like a nuclear explosion (on the Television)" Musharraf recorded in his memoirs (In the Line of Fire, pp. 200-201), "The enormity of the event was palpable. The world's most powerful country had been attacked on its own soil, with its own aircraft missiles. This was a great tragedy, and a great blow to the superpower". "America" he said, "was sure to react violently, like a wounded bear if the perpetrator turned out to be Al-Qaeda, then that wounded bear would come charging straight toward us. Al-Qaeda was based in neighbouring Afghanistan under the protection of those international pariahs, the Taliban. Not only that, we were the only country to maintain diplomatic relations with the Taliban and their leader, Mullah Omar." "September 11", he added, "marked an irrevocable turn from the past into unknown future. The world would never be the same."

Musharraf was advised by the foreign office to issue a statement. He wrote one (statement) quickly and said on national television that "we condemned this vile act, that we were against all forms of terrorism and stood with America at this appalling time, and that we would assist it any way we could." This was not good enough for the USA. Next day he was called out from a meeting to attend to a call from General Collin Powel, the US secretary of state. Musharraf found his distinguished caller "quite candid" who came straight to the point and demanded, "You are with us, or against us"? The Pakistan Dictator recognised this as "a blatant ultimatum", but kept his cool. He told General Powel that "we were with the United States against terrorism, having suffered from it and would fight along with his country against it." He further claimed that "we did not negotiate anything." The truth is that Powel left no room for such niceties. According to Musharraf he was told by his Director general of ISI who happened to be in Washington about his meeting with the U.S. deputy secretary of state, Richard Armitage, and reported that "not only that we had to decide whether we were with America, or with the terrorists, but that if we chose the terrorists we should be prepared to be bombed back to the Stone Age." However, Armitage has categorically denied that the he used such harsh words to threaten Pakistan.

Kamran Shafi in his perceptive piece titled 'Making Sense of It All' (*Dawn* dated 1/11/2010) exposed Musharraf dubious and vicious game plan. He wrote. "When Musharraf made his U-turn on the Taliban upon American 'urging' after 9/11, some of us thought he meant it. And, being the boss of bosses of the establishment of the Land of the Pure, would influence the Pakistani Deep State to change its stance too, and help the rest of the world fight the scourge wholeheartedly. And that the Taliban could do little against the rest of the world if no foreign power helped them. Consider: the Russians, the Central Asian Republics, China, Iran, all the countries surrounding Afghanistan except for some extremist elements in Central Asia and Pakistan were against the Taliban. They were isolated and could easily have been eliminated". A sincere and honest commitment to combat terrorism was farthest from Musharraf's mind. "Little did we know", Shafi wrote that "Musharraf and his junta did not mean what they said; that they were being two-faced; that the Deep State, with his approval, wanted to keep the Afghan Taliban as their proxies in the ongoing Great Game in Afghanistan, and their cousins, the Pakistani version of the blood-thirsty lot, as its 'strategic assets' against India." This indeed was the crux of commando Musharraf's strategic thrust. Shafi had hit the bull's eye.

His perception on another count was equally accurate. "While his (Musharraf) junta milked the Americans of billions of dollars", Kamran wrote "it allowed the Afghan Taliban to maintain their safe houses and bases inside Pakistani territory where they repaired after effectively targeting our 'allies' in Afghanistan and inflicting damage on coalition troops. This was two-facedness of a particularly vicious kind, but one that the Americans naively ignored, as it now turns out, to their cost." Musharraf indeed went to the extreme. He authorised base to "Quetta Shoura" and safe-housing of "Osama-bin-Laden in Abbotabad". This was ultimate in treachery.

According to a despatch by Indo-Asian News Service (December 24, 2011) datelined Washington, former Gen. Zia ud-din Butt appointed by Nawaz Sherif as army chief, to replace

Musharraf told a conference on Pakistani-US ties in October 2011 that according to his knowledge the then director general of Intelligence Bureau, Brigadier (retd.) Ijaz Shah, had "kept Osama-bin-Laden in an Intelligence Bureau safe house in Abbottabad." Osama bin Laden was gunned down May 2011 by US commandos in a daring operation using stealth helicopters.

The report claimed that "stunning revelation was unreported for some time as some intelligence officers had asked journalists not to publish Butt's remarks." The report said Butt told the daily *Dawn* Dec. 11 that he fully believed that "(Brigadier) Ijaz Shah had kept this man (bin Laden in the Abbottabad compound) with the full knowledge of General Pervez Musharraf..."

Brigadier Shah was the Intelligence Bureau chief during Musharraf's rule. He is believed to be the handling officer of the British-born terrorist Omar Sheikh, since convicted for the murder of *Wall Street Journal* reporter Daniel Pearl. Moreover, Benazir Bhutto had accused Shah of conspiring with terrorists to assassinate her. She had even named him in a letter as someone who should be investigated if she was killed. Musharraf still kept him in charge of Bhutto's security detail which "failed" to protect her, on the night of her assassination in 2007. Significantly, Shah left Pakistan for Australia after the assassination.

Earlier in 2004, President Musharraf nominated him to be High Commissioner to Australia. The nomination was believed to have been rejected by Canberra on account of his suspected links to terrorists.

Zia-ud-Din may have reasons to bad mouth Musharraf but the fact remains that world's most wanted fugitive terrorist had been living in a custom-built luxury complex in the garrison town of Abbottabad since 2005. The location was only 800 yards from the Pakistan military academy and hardly 50 kilometres from capital town of Islamabad. Given the mechanics of governance and power configuration in Pakistan this was only possible with official sanction, which had to have the crucial nod from the man at the very top—General Parvez Musharraf.

Indo-Pak Relations

General Musharraf recognised the diplomatic and other related statecraft imperatives of engaging with Indian leadership as well as building personal rapport with his Indian counterpart. At the same time, he was also painfully conscious of the difficulties in the way of developing such relations . His refusal to be part of the reception committee formed by Prime Minister Nawaz Sherif to welcome Atal Bhari Vajpayee on his peace mission to Pakistan because it would have required him to salute "the Prime Minister of the enemy country" was fresh in public memory. He was also known to have approved the "purification" of *Mazar-i-Quid Azim* after it was "polluted" by Vajpaye's visit. He was self confessed author of the Kargil conflict initiated just after the Lahore Peace Summit earlier that year. Musharraf was, therefore, to put it mildly regarded with scepticism in India. It may be rewarding to note that despite all the drama and bonhomie with Indian leadership, political class, civil society and media caricatured by Musharraf during his stint as Chief Executive/ President of Pakistan, his hatred of India remained undiminished. The evidence is there in black and white in his memoirs 'In the Line of Fire, p. 104)'. After the plane carrying him from Sri Lanka to Karachi on the fateful day of October 12, 1999 was barred from landing at Karachi airport and the plane was running out of fuel, a desperate Musharraf had the following conversation with the pilot. "Where can we go? I asked. "He said he could go to either Ahmedabad in India, or Oman, but we had to decide immediately because we were fast running out of fuel". "Over my dead body will you go to India, I declared angrily." His, on the spur of the moment response conformed to his known views about India... But the well considered and deliberate decision to flaunt his hatred of India so blatantly by putting it into print at leisure speaks volumes. And yet he had to find a way to establish contact with his Indian counterpart. The Gujarat earthquake in early 2001 offered the opportunity. "I telephoned Prime Minister Vajpaye to offer my sympathy and Pakistan sent relief goods including medicines" recalled Musharraf in his memoirs (In the Line of Fire p. 297). The configuration of stars seemed to favour Musharraf.

Prime minister Atal Bihari Vajpayee confounded both his friends and foes by extending an invitation to General Musharraf who had appointed himself President of the Islamic republic of Pakistan to visit India from 14 to 16 July, 2001. The historic Agra city was to be the venue of the meeting. What motivated Vajpayee to take a massive U-turn in country' foreign policy vis-à-vis Pakistan and invite the belligerent Pakistani General to a 20-Gun salute in "the enemy country " remained a mystery. Various theories continue to make the rounds. Some argue that Vajpayee acted under US pressure". Others claim that he was motivated by the obsession to gain immortality by resolving the intractable "Kashmir dispute" and earn a Nobel prize in the bargain. And so on.

For Generel Musharraf, the invitation could not have come at a more favourable time. It lent him and his regime not only legitimacy but also respectability. It indicated a significant turn about in Indian policy on Pakistan. India resiled from the position of no negotiation with the military regime. The pre-condition of holding negotiations with Pakistan only after the cross-border terrorism was halted was given up. By 'extending an invitation to the Pak President on his own, the Indian Prime Minister conceded that talks and proxy war in J&K could be pursued side by side.

Vajpayee-Musharraf engagement in Agra proved a disaster. After a good dose of theatricals and suspense the summit ended on an acrimonious note. Musharraf left in a huff. What exactly happened behind closed doors especially in five one to one rounds remained shrouded in secrecy even though both Musharraf and Vajpayee had given their versions. Musharraf would have us believe that the joint declaration "contained a condemnation of terrorism and recognition that the dispute over

Kashmir needed resolution in order to improve bilateral relations...The draft was very well worded and acceptable to both of us. We were approaching the climax of our visit [but Indians backed out]. "Indians", he says, "also backed out of an agreed redrafted version" (In the Line of Fire, p. 298). "Come on General, you cant' be serious. Drafting of a declaration embodying condemnation of terrorism and recognition of Kashmir dispute needed resolution, could neither be the ground for grounding the Summit, nor require three hours of intense haggling over words and sentences. "

"I told him (Vajpayee) bluntly", he goes on, "that there seemed to be some one above the two of us who had the power to overrule us. I also said that today both of us have been humiliated. He just sat there speechless". (In the Line of Fire p. 299). This was contested by Vajpayee. Expressing his surprise over the remark made by Pakistan President Pervez Musharraf that both of them felt insulted at the Agra summit, the former prime minister of India said, "No one insulted the General and certainly no one insulted me."

The former prime minister attributed the failure of the Agra summit to Musharraf position that bloodshed in J-K was "people's battle for freedom". India, on the other hand, believed there could be no normalcy in its relations with Pakistan until cross-border terrorism ended. Vajpayee said Musharraf took the stand that the violence taking place in Jammu and Kashmir "could not be described as terrorism". "He continued to claim that the bloodshed in the state was nothing but the people's battle for freedom. It was this stand of General Musharraf that India just could not accept," Vajpayee said, "and this was responsible for the failure of the Agra summit "(*PTI,* 26 July, 2007). It appeared neither of them was telling the whole truth. The somewhat simplistic versions proffered by both Musharraf and Vajpayee did not pass muster.

The approval of the Joint Declaration enthused President Musharraf so much that everything around smelled rosy. He even found "the hotel staff and all delegates truly exuberant" as if they were privy to what had transpired in the summit. He appeared to be supercharged with a kind of energy that comes only out of an unmitigated and unexpected windfall. Contrast this with the haste, huff and bitterness with which Musharraf departed after agreement eluded even on the revised draft. His omission to pay obeisance at the Ajmer Sharif holy shrine confirmed that he grossly resented being "cheated" of the gains secured in the form of the initial Joint Declaration, obviously to the detriment of Indian national interests. The hectic activity in India's corridors of power, the unscheduled entry of Sushma Swaraj in the venue of the Summit and intervention of Lal Krishan Advani confirmed the premise. The subsequent allusion to an 'invisible hand by Musharraf's spokesperson lent it further credence.

Even-though a national disaster was averted, the Indian leadership refused to learn any lesson. The handling of Indo-Pak relations since 1999 evidenced that detection and abortion of the Agra trap did not deter either the NDA government, or its UPA successors from merrily walking into other traps laid by Musharraf.

The summit invitation by which New Delhi accorded him legitimacy was fully utilised by Musharraf to "usurp the presidency, demonstrate his diplomatic skills and shed his quasi-pariah international status." He gladdened the hearts of extremist elements home by openly accusing the host nation, that, too, in the middle of a summit, of atrocities in Kashmir and pre-emptive capture of the Siachin Glacier. From Agra the commando President returned to Pakistan stronger. Hereafter he firmly retained the initiative in driving Indo-Pak parleys and practically dictated the course of events.

Any hope of India breaking the logjam on the assumption of power by UPA dashed to the ground when Manmohan Singh, the successor Prime Minister in the UPA comfortably slipped into Vajpayee's meandering policy mode on Pakistan. The first Musharraf - Manmohan Singh meeting took place in New York on 24 September, 2004 when the Indian Prime Minister called on the Pakistan President at his hotel. "It was an extremely pleasant encounter. I found the Prime Minister a very positive and genuine person with a desire to resolve disputes with Pakistan and establish good relation with us" wrote Musharraf in his memoirs (In the Line of Fire, p. 300). The quest for immortality via resolution of Kashmir tangle with Nobel Prize thrown in for international recognition bug appeared to have also latched on to the new incumbent of the Race course house.

Their one to one dialogue on 18 April, 2005 in Delhi after watching the match between Indian and Pakistan cricket teams to which Manmohan Singh had invited President Musharraf marked the Indian retreat from its long held strong position on Kashmir. The "Attot Aang" mantra was given a go by and the Parliament's unanimous 1994 resolution mandating the government of India to get occupied Jammu & Kashmir territories vacated from Pakistan's illegal occupation rendered irrelevant and meaningless. "We both agreed that we had to resolve the dispute and that we needed to find a solution "outside the box" wrote Musharraf "In the Line of Fire". And significantly added, "The prime minister did say that he could not agree to redrawing of borders, while I said I could not agree to accepting the Line of Control as permanent. " Prime Minister Manmohan Singh's 'objection' to redrawing of borders notwithstanding, India was not known to have raised the issue of POJK and Gilgit Baltistan at any of the subsequent negotiations at any level. This tended to support the widely prevailing perception that India had, in fact, offered to make the LOC permanent which Musharraf "tactically declined to concede" at that stage. Otherwise where was the provocation for Musharraf to record his rejection of making LOC permanent? It was also believed that in Track 11 engagements "Permanent LOC theme" was repeatedly played out. The Government of India must, therefore, clarify and state their position unambiguously. Otherwise it would be taken that something sinister was cooking behind the back of Indian people involving surrender to Pakistan the huge chunk of national territory of

Jammu & Kashmir illegally occupied by her through blatant aggression.

Musharraf thereafter pressed on with the advantage through rolling out series of proposals for resolution of Jammu & Kashmir problem. It may be emphasised that while influential political and media lobbies have been peddling the Musharraf "proposals" as credible peace initiatives by Pakistan worthy of serious consideration and projecting the Pak Dictator as a "Man of peace", the official spokesperson of Pak External Affairs ministry periodically reiterated that "the Government of Pakistan was committed to providing moral, political and diplomatic support to the Kashmiri people freedom struggle and the resolution of the Kashmir issue in accordance with the UN resolutions and the aspirations of the people of Kashmir." That this moral, diplomatic and political support was the cover for cross-border terrorism, or call it proxy war if you will, was well known the world over. Incidentally, the current prime minster of Pakistan Raja Ashraf repeated this mantra immediately after President Zardari retuned home signalling a thaw in relations between two countries and "generating a climate conducive to pursuance of the peace process between two countries."

Addressing a group of newspaper editors at an *Iftar* party in Islamabad on October 25, 2004, President General Musharraf suggested identification of various zones of "the disputed territory" followed by their demilitarisation and a determination of their status. In this most talked about proposal for resolution of J&K tangle, he divided Jammu & Kashmir state into the following seven regions.

1. POJK.
2. Gilgit Baltistan.
3. Jammu, Sambha and "Katwa" where Hindus are in majority.
4. Dodha, Phirkuch and Rajouri where Muslim population is in majority which includes Gujars, Sidhans and Rajas who are also associated with *Azad* Kashmir.

5. Kashmir Valley which also has Muslim majority.
6. Kargil which has Shia and Balti population in majority.
7. Ladakh and adjoining areas where Buddhists live.

President Musharraf further said that "it was imperative that the linguistic, ethnic, religious, geographic, political and other aspects of these seven regions should be reviewed and a peaceful solution to the problem found."

The proposal was rejected by opposition parties in Pakistan. President Musharraf call for open discussion on Kashmir was termed by the Pakistani Opposition parties as a "roll back." India on the other hand found it unacceptable as it envisaged redrawing of the territorial map in Jammu & Kashmir.

Implementation of the Musharraf proposal inherently involved partition of Jammu & Kashmir on communal lines. The other factors like language, ethnicity were mentioned for effect, to lend it respectability and make it palatable to the gullible lobby in India. The proposal to divide Jammu into three regions (Doda. Pooch Rajouri) and Ladakh into two (Leh and Kargil) on communal basis was patently mischievous.

Making a *suo moto* statement in Indian Parliament on foreign policy related issues, Prime Minister Manmohan Singh said that during his meeting with Pakistan President Pervez Musharraf in New York in September 2004, they had agreed that "possible options for a peaceful, negotiated settlement of the JK issue should be explored in a sincere spirit and a purposeful manner. The Indian Prime Minister asserted that "I made it clear to President Musharraf that while we are willing to look at various options, we would not agree to any redrawing of boundaries, or another partition".

Even otherwise, this Musharraf formula suffered from fatal flaws, factual inaccuracies and misrepresentations intended to lead to erroneous conclusions. His scheme, totally excluded from reckoning the Hindu majority district of Udhampur in Jammu region with an area of 4,550 sq. kms. and population of five lacs, fifty four thousand nine hundred eighty nine (5,54989).

As far as Muslim majority districts in Jammu region were concerned, Doda (the old district since divided into three districts of Ramban, Kishtwar and Doda) and the Rajouri have more than 40 per cent non-Muslim population with large contiguous Hindu majority pockets. In fact, in Tehsil Paddar in Doda (now Kishtwar district) Hindu population is around 98 per cent. Moreover Rajputs (Rajas in Musharraf's terminology) are ethnically an extension of Dogra identity. Gujars are spread over the entire Jammu region and constitute significant population in both regions of Kashmir and Jammu. Term Sudhans (Sidhins) merely refers to place of residence, Sudhonti in POK. All Sudhans were not Muslims. There are Hindu and Sikh Sudhans also.

An anti-climax in the high profile widely publicised Musharraf antics in the realm of Indo-Pak relation especially the resolution of the "Kashmir issue" arrived when Musharraf announced that he had been merely "floating ideas" to be discussed. The final and formal burial to Musharraf exertions was given by Foreign Minister Shah Mehmood Qureshi when he trashed former President Pervez Musharraf's four point formula saying it was "his thinking" which did not have the endorsement of Parliament, or Cabinet". His speech in the National Assembly on 5th May was much more strongly worded and categorical. "Musharraf's policies had extensively harmed the Kashmir cause", he said and added, "We are trying our level best to overcome the loss inflicted over Kashmir during the previous government". "Kashmir", Quershi declared, "has been the keystone of foreign policy of Pakistan and we will continue the diplomatic and moral support of the Kashmiri people."

Though somewhat belated, India's principled and constitutional position on Jammu and Kashmir was categorically and forthrightly reiterated by the Defence Minister AK Antony's in the Parliament on August 13, 2012. "A part of the territory of the State (Jammu & Kashmir) is under illegal and forcible occupation of Pakistan. The issue that remains to be resolved is the vacation by Pakistan of the area under its illegal occupation," he declared. This was in conformity with the 22nd February, 1994 unanimous Parliament resolution calling upon the Government of India to get vacated all the Jammu & Kashmir territories illegally occupied by Pakistan through aggression. Hopefully, India will stick to this position during the course of future negotiations.

PART II: A. THE MUSHARRAF ERA

(PUBLISHED ARTICLES)

8

General Musharraf; Challenges and Responses

1. The Agra Summit

The Vajpayee-Musharraf summit is on. Musharraf, who has donned the mantle of Presidentship of Pakistan, would be in India from July 14 to 16th. The historic city of Agra will be the venue of the meeting between the Prime Minister of India, Atal Bihari Vajpayee and the President of Pakistan. They will address some of the thorniest and challenging problems bedevilling the relations of the two neighbours. The meeting was mostly to one to one.

According to Major General Rashid Qureshi, the spokesman for General Musharraf, "the General is going to India with an open mind and have no objection to whatever India wants to discuss," Pakistan Foreign Secretary Inamul Haq added another dimension by stating that Pakistan would not insist on any pre-condition for the inclusion of Kashmir during the coming Vajpayee-Musharraf talks if India considered it as the "main hurdle". The summit between Indian Prime Minister and the Pakistan President will, it seems have no formal agenda. Positively viewed, this leaves lot of room for manoeuvre for the two leaders. Negatively, it signals failure to arrive at an agreement on the items to be included in the agenda.

If Vajpayee invited Musharraf to India "to walk the high road to fight our common enemy, the poverty," Musharraf expressed the hope to change the course of the history. Observers believe that the posturing of high ideas and good intentions were mostly cosmetic. Different statements emanating from Delhi and Islamabad testify to this reality. A mere mention by Musharraf of flexibility in approach raised so many eyes-brows in his county that he had to back track defensively like a child caught in some naughty act. Asked what he meant by 'flexible approach', he fumbled and said, "I suppose the word flexibility is creating confusion. Let me say that my openness of mind in talks with Indian Prime Minister would be directly proportionate to the openness the other side shows." "So it is not possible to clearly lay down the line of flexibility", he added. On the other hand, the statement of Foreign Minister Jaswant Singh that the entire state of Jammu & Kashmir is integral part of India has been endorsed by the Prime Minister. Not to be left behind, Musharraf told veteran Pak politician Nawabzada Naser Ullah Khan that "the Government would not back track from Pakistan's principled stand on the issue of Kashmir." Foreign Minister Abdul Sattar is again harping on the demand to include the Hurriyat in the talks, which he is fully aware are only bilateral in nature. Apparently, Pakistan Government wants to prop up the Hurriyat's absurd claim to be the sole voice of the people of Jammu & Kashmir.

Distancing himself from General Musharraf's position that Kashmir will be the core issue at the Summit, Prime Minister Vajpayee said, "Kashmir will be one of the various issues that will be discussed during the talks." He also asserted that the issue of Pakistan occupied Kashmir would also be discussed with General Musharraf at the Summit which was aimed at achieving "tension free relations". Alarmed Musharraf spoke to Vajpayee on phone and both promptly agreed to tone down the political rhetoric.

Qazi Hussain, the JEI Chief had earlier taken a some-what favourable view of the then Pakistan Chief Executive's visit to

India. However, in a hundred eighty-degree turn he openly questioned his credentials to speak on behalf of Pakistan, whose reins he had assumed through back door. Notwithstanding this political ping-pong, the euphoria amongst the common people regarding the Agra summit persists.

Contrary to the general belief in this country, Pakistanis are far from unanimous about the road to progress and prosperity that the nation must travel. The young generation educated and exposed to modernisation and globalisation, for instance, are keen of finding ways and means of ensuring well being of the common man in Pakistan through improving their quality of life. They are looking for space on the globalisation bandwagon rather than waste their time and energy on pursuing old animosities and settling senseless scores. They have no interest in nurturing the bitterness of the past and pursuing the "Hate India Campaign". They perceive the obscurantist fundamentalism and the cult of Jihad as greatest obstacles to the achievement of these goals. They are aware that peace is prerequisite to prosperity in Pakistan and view Vajpayee-Musharraf parlays in this context. They are intensely patriotic and would welcome only an arrangement that is fair, equitable and reasonable.

Intellectuals, progressive elements in Pak-society, Human Rights Activists and Captains of industry fully support the process of reconciliation between the two neighbours. They expected the engagement to produce a congenial atmosphere and promote understanding which may resolve long pending disputes between the two countries. Expectation from the Summit in this sense ran high. A thaw in the tension, they believed will help promote greater economic, cultural and social intercourse to the benefit of both countries.

On the other side of the social divide stood arrayed Pan Islamic fundamentalists committed to obscurantism, fanaticism and the cult of Jihad. They vehemently oppose the dialogue process. The Lashkar e Toiba declared that operations in Kashmir would continue despite the Indo-Pak summit. It vowed to carry on its activities evenif the Pakistan government were to impose a ban on it. Talks have taken place in the past also and will continue to be held in future. But the process of dialogue has nothing to do with the ongoing Jihad in Kashmir "declared Dawa-ul-Irshad Chief Hafiz Sayeed. The Hizabual Mujahadeen Supremo Silah-ud-din and other terrorist leaders have echoed similar sentiments. There was no ambiguity with regard to their stand which only hardened after the Summit was decided upon.

The Agra engagement, influential circles in Pakistan believed could mark the beginning of an era of prolonged and torturous negotiations that will run into difficulties from time to time. At that stage the United States, however will inevitable intervene to save the peace process. The third party intervention for which Pakistan had been trying so hard and for so long would thus be achieved.

What is General Musharraf upto?

When Pakistan President General Musharraf ditched the Afghan Taliban and their Pan-Islamic patrons in January, he was responding to domestic as well as international concerns. His decision to hitch his wagon to the global anti-terrorist coalition, crafted and led by the United States of America, was similarly guided. An ethnically divided, politically fractured and economically paralysed Pakistan bleeding from sectarian violence in any case had little option. The post-September scenario provided a God-sent opportunity for Pakistan to reoccupy the centre-stage in the American game-plan in the region. This tie-up with the anti-terrorist coalition was fully backed by the powerful feudal lobby that controls and manipulates all the levers of power in that country—political, administrative, economic and military.

Musharraf's January address had two clearly defined components. First, make the world believe that he meant to effectively curb the Pan-Islamic terrorist outfits, reform and control management of *madrasas* that manufactured terrorists and ensure that the soil of Pakistan was not used for exporting terrorism. The euphoria thus generated would make the USA and other major powers insensitive to the implications of the other crucial declaration that Pakistan "will continue to extend moral and diplomatic support to the 'freedom struggle in Kashmir". That by 'moral and diplomatic support' Musharraf implied sustaining cross-border terrorism in Jammu and Kashmir was public knowledge. It was equally obvious that to export terrorism, it had to be first bred in Pakistan. A country breeding terrorism on her soil undoubtedly ran the risk of exposing her political, social and military systems to the lethal contamination. The United States Government repeatedly certified the sincerity of Musharraf's 'assurances' regarding 'the posturing on Kashmir. It was manifestly tactical. There was enough evidence to support this assumption.

By January, Pervez Musharraf made it appear all was set to banish fundamentalist control over the *madrasas* that bred *jehadis.* Instead of initiating effective measures, he opted to engage in somewhat facile behind-the-scene negotiations with the *Mullahs*. This resulted in the surrender of the 'precious initiative' and provided the *Mullahs* time and space to recover and regroup. The establishment took more than six months to promulgate an ordinance to regulate the functioning of the *madrasas,* 'teaching' about six lakh students including fifteen thousand foreigners. The ordinance prescribed that contravention of the provisions of the ordinance will attract closure of the *madrasas,* or a fine, or both. Interestingly, the ordinance also informed that 'the details of the fine are being worked out. Further comments regarding the seriousness of action in this critical area would be superfluous.

The Pakistan Minister for Religious Affairs significantly stated in a PTV discussion that the ordinance contained nothing new. "The provisions already existed in various laws and have only been compacted for the facility of enforcement." He also assured the *Mullahas* that "the government did not intend to interfere with the autonomy of the management of the institutions". Eventhough the General's thunder ended in a whimper, the Ithad-e-Tanzeemat, an alliance of organisations representing about 8000 *madrasas* in Pakistan, is on the war-path. They have now threatened to come out on the roads if the regulations were not abandoned. The main bone of contention, interestingly, was the source of their funding, which they stubbornly refuse to disclose.

The action against *jehadi* leadership after Musharraf's January speech was similarly lukewarm and cosmetic. Arrests were made but no evidence adduced. Detentions were ordered under laws that mandated release after a brief spell in jail unless certain conditions were met. In the absence of any follow-up by the authorities, a majority of the detainees, especially those who mattered, were set free. Musharraf's deeds don't match his words. Or is the General developing cold feet?

Noted political commentator, Khaled Hussain, writing from Washington in a recent issue of *Times* quotes a leading US expert on South Asia as saying: "The USA is said to be privately distressed at Musharraf's actions and his failure to have delivered on his promises. Washington feels that the General has neither staged a meaningful crackdown on terrorism, nor liberalised his regime, nor acted to put a complete end on what India calls "cross-border terrorism". "So far," he says, "publicly, Washington has been expressing its appreciation for Musharraf but tensions are building among policy and decision-makers as to what extent and for how long Musharraf can be defended, or supported. "

It is obvious that the United States is avoiding to go public with her concerns about Musharraf's double-speak. India seems to be inhibited by diplomatic niceties and merely insists upon its implementation of Musharraf's pledge, on the ground. In Pakistan, intellectuals, thinkers media persons and concerned citizens have, however, been more frank, honest and candid. Pakistani nuclear physicist Parvez Hoodbhoy, for instance, addressed the issue of Musharraf's duplicity squarely. "To run with the hares and hunt with the hounds—and imagine that the world will not know has become impossible," he bluntly stated in his write-up in *Dawn* (May 28, 2002). "Today," he said, "in spite of General Musharraf's soothing statements, there is little doubt that militant camps shelter under Pakistan's nuclear umbrella. Having operated openly for over a decade in full public view and with obvious state backing, only magic, or a massive military action can eliminate them." The General, obviously, possesses no magical skills. And there is no trace of "massive military action" against domestic terrorism.

The Pakistan President's policy-dilemma is best summed up by noted columnist Khaled Hussain. "The task of cleaning up Pakistan," he wrote in *Friday Times,* "is a colossal one. The *jehad* was generated with many years' effort at the expense of the state sovereignty. To roll it back and to regain internal sovereignty is going to take many years and General Musharraf knows he can't do it in his short tenure. There are far too many vested interests attached to this phenomenon, and the state is used to cooperating with it. "

Whatever his compulsions, or motivation, Musharraf shocked the world community, particularly the United States, by openly repudiating 'assurances to permanently end cross-border tension' given to the United States of America. In an interview to the *Newsweek* last June, the Pakistan President flatly denied having given any such "assurance." "I have told President Bush, nothing is happening across the Line of Control. This is the assurance I have given," and added, "I am not going to give you an assurance that for years nothing will happen..." The United States was quick to come out with a categorical contradiction. The State Department spokesman, Richard Boucher, said on June 25 that "Deputy Secretary Armitage was given assurances by President Musharraf on June 6 for ending infiltration across the Line of Control permanently. These assurances were also given the Secretary of State, and the President of the United State in their conversations as well as repeatedly to our representatives, our charge and our ambassador in Islamabad. The Pakistan President was reported to have 'privately' assured the Bush Administration as late as on June 24, 2002 that he will indeed enforce a permanent end to infiltration from the Pak occupied Kashmir (PoK) into the Valley. So what exactly is he up to? Musharraf's latest 'constitutional acrobatics' are clearly meant to strengthen his own position, the position of a General whose moral authority has been severely eroded by a 'sham referendum'. According to Ayaz Amir, the referendum "was a gift from the Gods for the people of Pakistan for it achieved the impossible, reducing the level of arrogance and cockiness flying about in Islamabad. Referendum *say pehley* (before referendum) and referendum kay *baad* (after referendum) are two different stories". If the truth be told, there are hardly any takers for Musharraf's boast that 'he was going to be around to serve Pakistan for a long time to come'. The October deadline, mandated by the country's Apex Court, the formidable mainstream political parties line up against him, and Opposition by the religious parties combine spell his doom. The Pakistan Army top brass are said to be in no mood to be seen as 're-enforcing failure', that would be a cardinal violation of military strategy. This leaves Musharraf with two viable options. First, to heed to the Pakistani nuclear scientist Parvez Hoodbhoy's forthright advise *(Dawn,* May 28), "Whatever Pakistan might choose to think," he wrote, "the rest of the world remains incredulous of the continuing official Pakistan position that it provides 'only diplomatic and moral support' to the people of Kashmir. Earlier denials of military involvement in Kargil, or of providing military support to the Taliban regime have hugely diminished Pakistan' international credibility." And significantly added, "It is now a matter of survival for Pakistan to visibly demonstrate that it has severed all links with the militant groups it had formerly supported, to be firm about providing 'only diplomatic and moral support' and to implement what General Musharraf promised in his January speech." This was a sensible piece of advice suggesting an honourable course of action. This could restore the credibility of Pakistan in the world community and open up avenues for resolution of many daunting problems between India and Pakistan. Failing that Musharraf may be compelled to follow the route recommended by Ayaz Amir in his write up titled 'Pakistan's crisis of destiny' *(Dawn)*. "*You* have sat too long here for any good you have done," he quoted from the famous address by Cromwell to the long parliament, "depart I say, and let us have done with you. In the name of God, Go."

Musharraf Ko Gussa Kiyon Aaya

Pakistan President Musharraf is angry. He is angry because his well-crafted ploy on Jammu and Kashmir fell flat. His 25 October, 2004 Islamabad *Iftar* party outpourings on Jammu and Kashmir packaged as 'food for thought' were, he himself stressed, meant for "national debate". The agencies reported on 26, October that the Pakistan President called upon "the nation to debate his options before Pakistan presents a new position before India". This was obviously a strategic move through the media aimed at provoking India into a discussion without committing Pakistan to any particular course of action. Through this device the reaction at home could be minimised and the door left ajar for retreat, if necessary.

As if on cue, the debate instantly spilled over to Kashmir where both factions of the Hurriyat dutifully made favourable noises. Even Ali Shah Gellani's Hurriyat, whose leader was literally wedded (in a traditional Hindu marriage with no option for divorce) to the UN resolutions and the "Right of self-determination" said, "These suggestions could be discussed in a tripartite forum of dialogue where India, Pakistan and Kashmiris could sit on table and discuss the possible solutions." Good friend Richard Armitage, the US Deputy Secretary of State expectedly found the 'proposal' "interesting". This was sweet music to Musharraf's ears. Therefore, Delhi striking a discordant note by remaining calculatingly cool understandably bugged him. The General was perhaps not entirely to blame. The response from Delhi did not materialise on the expected lines. For long, Delhi had routinely obliged him through a running debate on whatever of significance, or otherwise he chose to convey through his media self-laudatory outbursts in which he usually blew hot and cold at the same time. The story made rounds that if General Musharraf were to sneeze in Islamabad, the NDA government would either instantly applaud the high musical quality of the sound produced, or pick the hot-line to Washington to complain of the threatening noise in violation of definite assurances conveyed through Armitage.

Indian foreign minister, Natwar Singh, responded to a media question abroad the aircraft returning home after attending the funeral of Yassar Arafat that India would listen to the proposals if given formally. This made Pakistan President-cum-Chief of the Army Staff furious. His retort from Lahore on 20th November, "it is not a song one has to listen. We expect to be talking. We expect answers", bears testimony to his anger. His body language on the TV screen spoke even more eloquently. Have a heart General, you surely do not expect the government of a sovereign country to recklessly rush into 'talking' about the 'food for thought' dished out by you after a sumptuous *Iftar* meal for the consumption of your own people and providing 'answers' to 'proposals' which actually were not proposals. Moreover, your own assertion that this 'food for thought' did not represent any shift in the "maximalist" position of Pakistan as you put it could hardly be expected to generate any enthusiasm in India. So, if you wish to 'talk' and 'expect answers', come out with formal structured proposals through internationally recognised channels and you will find India willing and ready to respond. 'And that is it. '

The 25th October 'food for thought' could be construed as part of General Musharraf's yet another 'peace diplomacy offensive', a stratagem through which he was generally perceived to have scored over India. He had, it was argued, succeeded to a large extent in convincing the West in general and the USA in particular of his 'flexible approach' and keenness to work out an equitable and enduring solution of the 'core issue' of Kashmir that had plagued the relations between the two nuclear powers of South Asia. The US had her own pressing compulsions to perpetuate the myth in her own national interest. She, on her part needed to humour, pamper and promote Musharraf with a view to strengthen his position in Pakistan that would keep the Pan-Islamists in that country at bay and facilitate Pakistan establishment's continuous and more vigorous participation in the war against international terror, especially in the context of reported presence of Osama bin Laden in area bordering Afghanistan. On his part, the General had always attempted to portray India as a somewhat reluctant player in the 'lofty' endeavour for finding a solution to the Kashmir issue and contributing in averting a disastrous confrontation in nuclear 'flash point in South Asia'. Now that Prime Minister Shoukat Aziz is in Delhi, let us see how the 'proposals' are presented in the light of Pakistan Foreign Minister Khurshid Mehmood Kasuri's statement that "our Prime Minister is going to India where the proposal will be discussed."

Musharraf's 'food for thought' refers to seven so-called regions that "constitute" the state of Jammu and Kashmir. Of these, he says, five were in the "Indian held Kashmir". On our side of the Line of Control there are only three well delineated and recognised regions; Ladakh, Kashmir and Jammu. So where are the two remaining regions? Musharraf's reference to religious identity of the regions provides a clue to the mischief to divide Jammu region on communal basis. In fact, almost all the solutions for the Jammu & Kashmir tangle projected by various 'think tanks' mostly from USA directly, or indirectly suggest division of Jammu region. It is heartening that the Prime Minister has categorically rejected any suggestion to divide the state, or regions on communal grounds. But this is not enough. The political and intellectual classes in Jammu region have to seriously grasp the implications of the vicious thrust. It is time they do some hard thinking on the dangers that loom large on the political horizon and hammer out a united response at least on this single but critical issue.

General Musharraf was reported to have told the visiting Indian journalists in Lahore on 20th November that he insisted on the inclusion of Hurriyat Conference (for whose re-unification his government is making desperate efforts) in dialogue for finding a solution of Kashmir imbroglio. "We want inclusion of Hurriyat Conference in the talks as they are the true representatives of the people of Kashmir", he pompously declared, Pray under what canons of international protocol has Pakistan appropriated the right to determine who should represent the people of Jammu and Kashmir if and when they become party to negotiations? Whom does the Hurriyat really represent and how has the representative character been determined? The fractured and truncated rag tag coalition of disparate groups and individuals thrown out by their parties do not even claim to represent Jammu and Ladakh. It is sad but true that Delhi has significantly contributed to the grossly out of proportion importance being accorded to the Hurriyat Conference. The Central governments past and present are known to be pampering the conglomerate knowing fully well that it was a creation of Pakistan and sustained through the help of OIC and Western powers. Ironically, the mainstream parties like National Conference, People's Democratic Party and the Congress who enjoy internationally recognised popular mandate were apologetic about their own representative character. The National Conference and the PDP were even competing with each other in espousing the cause of the Hurriyat in a manner that diluted their own credentials. The Government of India and the leadership of these parties need to seriously review their stances and take speedy and transparent corrective measures. The coming months are going to be crucial. Let Musharraf's tantrums not unduly influence either Indo-Pakistan peace process, or the quest for resolution of difficulties in Jammu and Kashmir. This was essential to keep both these processes on track and moving forward in the positive direction.

Can Musharraf Subdue Religious Extremism?

Pakistan President General Musharraf's January 12 "historic and path-breaking policy statement" was superbly crafted. It managed to address variety of concerns including those of India and the world public opinion while firmly retaining the focus upon the interests of Pakistan and the 'true sprit' of Islam. It was also a call to his fellow countrymen to jettison the back breaking and unsavory baggage of fundamentalism acquired since the days of Zia-ul-Haq. His crediting the *sufi* saints like Data Gunj Baksh for the spread of Islam was highly significant. It was almost a stroke of genius as the overwhelming majority of Pakistanis reveres them and follow their interpretation and practices of Islam. This preference is, in fact, a reflection of his own faith, whatever his political compulsions to ride piggy back on Islamic fundamentalists in Kashmir and Afghanistan. Remember his last visit to this country. In his engagement calendar, pilgrimage to the shrines of Hazrat Nizam-ud-din Aulia and Ajmer Shrief figured prominently. *Begum* Musharraf took the first opportunity to pay obeisance at the *dargah* of Khawaja Salim Christi at Agra. It is also interesting to note that after Musharraf's statement *'kafis'* of Bulley Shah have begun to increasingly find favour with Pakistan Television and Radio. It was a treat to listen to *bullia kee jana main kon*, the other day on PTV rendered with such intense fervour. Musharraf's interaction with religious scholars in a two-day conference in Islamabad on 17th and 18th of January is yet another significant landmark in which he emphasised that the reforms initiated by him were not opposed to the teachings of Islam. "We are opposed to those who blindly ape the West. At the same time we want to confront those on the other side of the spectrum, religious extremists", he said. And declared that "The middle path is the ideal option for Pakistan and we seek to promote it". "It may be recalled that Musharraf held extensive consultations with the Islamic clerics even before his 12th January address. Earlier addressing a *Seerat* Conference, he had debunked the Fundamentalist dream of a world being ruled by the Muslim *umah* citing facts and figures. The battle against the fundamentalist fringe in Pakistan, it appears, has been joined.

There is no dearth of people in and out of establishments in India and rest of the world who question both his intentions and ability to translate his policy statement into concrete action. Their premise hinged upon doubts in his capability to garner the support of the people of Pakistan in this revolutionary U-turn. They forget that Musharraf has already won the crucial round; his dumping of the Taliban in Afghanistan and joining the US-led world coalition against global terrorism.

Sufism received support of the vast 'silent majority'. The fundamentalist's dissenters merely succeeded in causing some noisy demonstrations involving a small segment of population. Since then the banned terrorist outfits both operating on the home turf and external fronts including J&K. His rejection of theocracy for Pakistan polity was accompanied by 'revolutionary'electoral reforms enabling Muslims and non-Muslims to vote for the same candidate. Sixty seats for women have also been reserved in the National Assembly. Maintaining the momentum of his thrust, Musharraf announced on 24th of January last in a conference on Human Development in Islamabad that 'Elections (to the Provincial and National Assemblies) will be held in October". UN Secretary General Kufi Annan was present on the occasion.

Musharraf's detractors in Pakistan and abroad were somewhat foxed by these totally unexpected moves. Former Prime minister Benazir Bhutto wrote in the *Gulf News,* Dubai, "Not one head has rolled for the past policies presently repudiated. Moreover, *madrassas* can be passed from one favoured group to another". She is deliberately ignoring the 'purges' in Pakistan military and civil establishment for reasons that are not far to seek. As far as the *madarssas* are concerned, Musharraf has not abolished the institutions. Benazir was, however, right when she said, *madarssas* can be passed from one to other favoured group. In fact, the Pakistan President had openly indicated what kind of *madarssas* would be favoured. In any case, it ill befitted Benazir who enthusiastically rode the Pan Islamic fundamentalist bandwagon in early nineties and outdid her predecessors in aggressive rhetoric on Kashmir to deliver sermons. On the other hand, Western observers appeared to be treating every *mullah* as a fundamentalist. They forget that the Islamic mainstream in the sub-continent had remained historically averse to fundamentalism, a concept alien to their religious, social and cultural ethos. *The Washington Post* (Jan. 20) quoted Abdul Aziz as saying, "Musharraf said Pakistanis are sick of religious intolerance", but he asked, "If people are sick of it, why are our mosques so full every Friday?" It is amazing that such a ridiculous viewpoint should have found space in the prestigious newspaper. Since when offering Friday prayers, mandatory for all Muslims to be offered *Ba jammat* (in congregation) had become a symbol of 'religious intolerance'.

It was important for us in India to realise that Musharraf's policy statement primarily addressed domestic concerns. Remember, Pakistan was at the brink of anarchy, its society badly fractured. The sectarian violence promoted by the extremists was tearing apart the very fabric of their Islamic entity. The army itself was being infected by the virus of fundamentalism. The rulers of a bankrupt soft Pakistan were themselves feeling threatened. The 11th September terrorist attack on the U S pride and world primacy changed every thing. The declaration of war on global Terror and its bastion Taliban-ruled Afghanistan, which sheltered the world's most wanted terrorist Osama bin Ladin and his harbourer Mullah Omar provided both the challenge and opportunity Musharraf made the best of it. He decided to go along with the global anti-terrorist coalition in Pakistan's national self-interest. Having overcome the Fundamentalist dissent and somewhat sporadic resistance to his anti-Tailbone stance, Musharraf seems to have felt emboldened to take on the extremists. This also explained his bold and courageous bid to change course in the direction mapped by the creator of Pakistan, Mohd. Ali Jinnah. In the process he had been able to address the anti-terrorist concerns of the world public opinion as well as the 'demands' made by India following the terrorist attack on Indian Parliament.

Support from two influential and powerful segments of Pakistan society brightened the chances of success of the new thrust. Feudalism still reigns supreme in Pakistan. The feudal elements control the crucial means of production like Agriculture and industry. Their dominance over country's defense services, bureaucracy and corridors of power is unchallenged. And they stand to lose all the power and privileges under a fundamentalist dispensation where under the sovereignty of the state is transferred to the *Ullema*. The educated youth of Pakistan whether from the upper strata of society, or belonging to ever expanding middle class are plugged into the global economic and commercial circuit. Improving the quality of life and achieving speedy upward mobility are the forces that drive them. The large Pakistani work force spread over Middle East, USA, UK and Europe, whose remittances home sustain larger number of families also export the dreams of prosperity and progress as part of single forward moving world economy. In a fundamentalist dispensation the women of Pakistan stand to lose the most. The horrors of the talibanised Afghanistan haunt them. Given their numerical strength and high stakes they can be expected to rally behind the movement towards a modern liberal state.

President Musharraf cleverly delinked the 'Kashmir Issue' from his fight against Islamist extremists and sectarian fanatics at home, Pakistan position on Kashmir remains unchanged. In his own word, "the moral, diplomatic and political support to the cause of Kashmiri's struggle for self-determination will continue". This in essence implies that even if there are effective curbs on cross-border terrorism by Pakistan, there may at the best be reversal to pre-1998 position but with the terrorist super structure intact. Given the trained manpower military hardware and communication network/equipment available with the terrorist groups', it is estimated that they were capable of sustaining themselves for two to three years. It would be reasonable to assume that financial and material support from across the borders will continue to come in may be at somewhat reduced scale.

We, in India should take a comprehensive and holistic view of the changes and challenges emerging on the social, religious, cultural and political landscape of Pakistan. As stable Modern and progressive Pakistan was clearly in our long-term interest. The dilemma, however, lies in reconciling the duty to defend the integrity of the country against secessionist terrorist in Jammu and Kashmir which Pakistan will continue to promote with need to 'encourage' the forces struggling for a non-theocratic, modern and liberal dispensation in that country. This was the challenge to the statecraft skills and diplomatic ingenuity of our rulers and the opposition leadership alike. The nation has to quickly come up with a concrete and viable response.

Disgraced Pak Dictator on Anti-India Propaganda Spree

Even in the cold, Musharraf has not lost his penchant for bluff and bluster. The deposed former dictator, a fugitive from justice in his own country, was hosted by a Indian national channel the other day perhaps in a quest for scoop and be the first to grab the controversial personality in the hope for sensational disclosures. The disgraced Pakistan ruler fully utilised the opportunity to propagate Pakistan's perverted version of events and justification for her anti-India policies.

He attempted to justify Pakistan's perennial military confrontation with India on the plea that his country was merely pursuing the policy of "Defence deterrence" forced upon her by a hostile India through deployment of a huge chunk of her army on the Pakistan borders. And to buttress his argument, he went on to reel off the number of Indian army divisions facing Pakistan leaving Pakistan no choice but to make suitably matching defensive deployment of her armed forces. Nothing could be farther from the truth but the person conducting the interview did not respond. The viewers were thus left with the impression that a valid point had been made.

History is witness that driven by anti-India paranoia and lust for Jammu & Kashmir territory Pakistan from the day one chose aggression as the sole tool to achieve her military and political objectives. Even before the ink had dried on the partition deed, Pakistan mounted the tribal invasion in Jammu & Kashmir, planned, provisioned and led by its army regulars. The fact that Pakistan regular army openly joined the aggression was admitted, recorded and authenticated. How can any reasonable person who claims to speak on behalf of his nation and country and the one who was a major player in the diabolical anti-India game-plans make such atrocious claim on a respected Indian channel, and more importantly, get away with it unquestioned and uncontested? Can wars of 1965, 1971 and the Kargil incursions not to mention the proxy war in Jammu & Kashmir which had by now extended its vicious reach to the entire country by an rational criteria even remotely be linked to a policy of defence deterrence"?

Musharraf accused Indian intelligence agency RAW of fomenting trouble in Balochistan. Musharraf said "he did not know if ISI was involved in terror, subversion and sabotage in India but he was certain of the involvement of the RAW in Balochistan. Striking a note of "reasonableness" he suggested that yes, if ISI was doing something wrong in India, both must stop.

What are the facts. Balochistan was a directly administered British territory without any political rights, or representation. It was arbitrarily assigned to the newly carved out dominion of

Pakistan by the departing British Imperial power. Indian National Congress was the sole party with political presence there led by Abdul Samad Khan Achakzai, also known as the Balouch Gandhi. The Baloach people were fiercely opposed to the pernicious "Two Nation Theory" on which the foundation of Pakistan was laid. The tribals and others, therefore, understandably opposed the arrangement and mounted stiff resistance against this switching over of masters from the British to Punjabis. Even the ruler of Kalat revolted. The state of Pakistan instead seeking understanding and conciliation reacted with brute military force including bombardment by the Pak Air Force.

Over the decades the severity of resistance fluctuated with changes of regimes in Pakistan but the conflict persisted. It was primarily driven by the tribal tradition of avenging the killing of their kin. Musharraf himself is accused of masterminding the assassinations of Nawab Akbar Bugti and Nawabzada Balach Mari, two eminent tribal leaders. Bugti was a former chief minister of Balochistan. Criminal cases have been registered against Musharraf in this connection. Only the other day, a conclave of Islamic scholars issued a *fatwa* declaring Musharraf "*wajib ul qatal*" (fit/marked for murder). This man had the audacity to accuse India of creating conflict in Balochistan from the Indian soil naming an organisation not-even conceived when the revolt erupted there. Interestingly, Musharraf was certain that the Indian intelligence agency was involved in Baloch resistance but he, a former chief of Pakistan Army and President / Chief Martial Law Administrator feigned 'ignorance' of the subversion and sabotage indulged in by the infamous Pak ISI, a matter of public knowledge. Wasn't Musharraf straining the public credulity beyond reason?

Musharraf unashamedly praised Lashkar-e-Toiba, named by the UN as a terrorist organisation involved in numerous acts of terrorism in India and other countries as "charity which had done a great job in organising relief in POK 2005 earthquake". He was unconcerned about its criminal role in 26/11 Mumbai outrage conclusively established after Headly disclosures. And for good reasons. After all the Lashkar was a strategic asset of Pakistan army which was largely responsible for keeping Kashmir terror pot boiling. Moreover, it was at Musharraf's behest that the LeT was inducted into the POK brushing aside the protests of the local population and objections of the POK government. There were allegations that huge funds donated by the world community for relief of quake victims were siphoned for the LeT for terrorist activities. The LeT had built a massive base in Muzaffarabad where its Petrol depot alone encompassed miles of land adjacent to the populated area. He justified lack of action against the terrorist activities of the Lashkar on the specious plea that the organisation "enjoyed lot of popular support" in Pakistan. The assertion speaks volumes for the state of governance and the rule of law in that country, the pace whereof was set by the discredited dictator himself. In any case, by whom and by what means the so called popularity of LeT in Pakistan had been assessed? Incidentally, credible surveys had established that over 90 per cent Pakistanis considered USA as enemy number one of Islamabad and demanded Pakistan have no truck with that country. Why did Musharraf and his successors not walk out of US coalition in response to the peoples sensitivities? It is indeed tragic that the uncontrovertibly facts were not put to him. A smug Musharraf wearing a mischievous smile departed from the screen happy and contended.

The Channel was denied any scope but ended up with becoming a conduit of disseminating un contested distortions of facts, pedalling of half truths and untenable assertions which could tempt the viewers to "see logic in their presentations" and develop scepticism about the validity and justification of own national policy. No input could be more precious for the Pakistani managers of Public Perception Management, a key thrust in the psychological warfare against India.

9

Trouble in Pakistan: Indian Concerns

Deadly Terror Cocktail Brewing in Pakistan

Indian Strategic, Economic and Technological Assets on the Radar

The Prime Minister's address to the Chief Ministers Conference on Internal Security in Delhi on 17th August, 2009 was both significant and startling. Its significance lay in sounding a timely note of warning to the national well as the international community that the ruling elite in Pakistan were promoting major and wider terrorist strikes against India from their soil, their public posturing to the contrary notwithstanding. It was starting, because Pakistan's political and military leadership had repeatedly stated that their real enemy was terrorism in the West, not India in the East. ISI Chief Lt. Gen. Pasha had gone to the extent of saying that "we in Pakistan are not stupid. We know the enemy is in the Western front where we are fighting terrorist and not India in the East." Sane elements across the national boundaries were hoping that given the precarious economic, security and deep social and political divide, the leadership will behave responsibly and sensibly. It was in Pakistan's own national interest to forge a relationship of understanding with India and work for a joint front against terrorism, both home grown and that of alien origin.

The major part of PM Manmohan Singh's speech only confirmed the ground realities and what we were writing and saying for the last about five years. The area of operations of terrorists' today extended far beyond the confines of Jammu & Kashmir and covered all parts of the country. The levels of infiltration which had come down very substantially witnessed a surge this year. The infiltrators appeared better equipped. There were signs of revival of overground activity and attempts were also being made to expliot isolated and unconnected incidents like the those in Shopian, Sopore and Baramulla to create an impression of grounds well of anti-India feelings. The PM did, however, drop a bomb shell when he said that "there is credible information of ongoing plans of Terrorist groups in Pakistan to carry out fresh attacks in India."

Even a cursory glance on the spread of terrorist strikes in the country in the recent past would confirm that the target zone extended to the entire country from Kashmir to Karnataka and Mumbai to Manipur with special focus on the National Capital Delhi, the commercial capital Mumbai and the Informational technology hubs like Banglore and Hyderabad. Investigation in number of cases had already revealed that some indigenous terror groups were looped into the Al-Qaeda network while the rest were handled by Al-Qaeda associates like LeT, Jaish-e-Mohammad and Huji. The existence of large number of "sleeper cells" was also no secret.

In fact, the latest intelligence suggested that the south may well be the favoured target this time around. It should be understood that the enemy was not aiming at, or expecting any quick startling strategic gains. The long term objective of the vicious game plan was to gradually subvert and sap the techno-economic strength of the country. This squarely jelled with Pakistan's unconcealed policy of "bleeding India by thousand cuts".

By the beginning of 2008, Pakistan's game plan of 1988-89 of securing the elimination of the pro-independence outfits like JKLF by pitting them against the Indian security forces and gradually starving them of financial and techno-military hardware back up was successfully completed. Pro-Pakistan gangs like Hizab-ul-Mujahieen in its various incarnations had occupied the space vacated by JKLF reinforced by LeT, Jaish, Huji etc. mainly exported from Pakistan. At present, they control the terror machine operating in Kashmir. Musharraf's categorical declaration that an Independent Kashmir was not at all an option removed even the fig leaf of *azadi* with which the real design for annexation of Kashmir by Pakistan was sought to be covered.

The vast majority of Muslims of Kashmir were disenchanted with the Jihad, aghast at the futility of enormous sacrifices and destruction of economic infrastructure and convinced that the combination of government of Pakistan and Jihadi Tanzeems lacked the capability to oust India from Kashmir. The fear of Jihadi gun worked no more. The open defiance of their diktat of boycott call of election after election illustrated the point. Local recruits for Jihad were scarce and reinforcement from across LoC to compensate for unacceptable causalities were increasingly difficult. The master terrorists in Islamabad could not help taking note of these harsh realties. According to reports a Strategy Review session was held in ISI HQs some time in the January-February 2008. After an in-depth analysis and detailed discussions, it was decided to cast the overground segment of the network in Kashmir in the pivotal role with the terrorists assigned the responsibility to provide back up so as to provide teeth to the street action. They were simultaneously to keep enacting terror strikes albeit of low cost variety to perpetuate the façade of continuing struggle for independence. In the meantime the operatives in Kashmir were assured that all out efforts would be made to push reinforcement and equipment across the LoC. What began with the sudden almost maniacal outburst on the non-issue of land use for the duration of the Yatra by the Shri Amarnath Shrine Board and had since been followed through 'Muzafrabad Chalo' to the incidents of Shopian, Sopore and Baramulla bears testimony to this strategy. A conspiracy of circumstances gifted them some issues but there should be no doubt that one, or other issue would have been found, an ordinary incident blown out of proportion or even fabricated to serve their purpose. The Indian security forces were the target of all these exertions with projection of the Indian State as the villain of the psieace. The frantic and enhanced efforts at infiltration by trained terrorists speak for themselves.

Apparently, the decision taken in early part of 2008 had now been reversed. Intelligence inputs suggest that the ISI faction co-ordinating Jihad in Kashmir had now directed the LeT, Jaish, HM and Al-Badr terrorist outfits to go full blast hitting targets all over India. Coming days were, therefore, likely to witness lot of action. Some indications of the breaking out of the terror storm were already visible. But whether the ISI- Pan Islamic terror groups combine actually succeeded in creating and exporting to India a terrorist storm of the dimensions they were working for would to a large extent depend upon how the equations between ISI factions play out in days to come. The situation will also be significantly impacted by he threat perception, the seriousness of the response and the quality of the counter strategy devised by India. There can therefore, really be no two opinions about the need and urgency for effective and urgent counter measures tailored/updated to thwart the enemy politico-strategic aims and neutralise the enormous mischief potential of its known indigenous assets.

The surg in infiltration from across the LoC/IB, this year and the latest developments confirmed the apprehension that the Anti-India elements hooked into the Pan-Islamic Fundamentalist terror machine and firmly ensconced in the power structure of Pakistan still called the shots on her eastern frontiers. The failure, or inability of the political government to demolish the training-infrastructure even with in the territory of Pakistan and continued presence of hundreds of fully trained and equipped terrorists in the Launching Pads along the LoC/IB awaiting chances and opportunity to cross over tellingly underscores the point. There were reports though not fully authenticated of a trade off between the pro-West and Jihadi factions with in Pakistan establishment to the effect that the Jihadis will support the war against Tehrik-e-Taliban in the West in exchange for freedom to persecute Jihad against India in Kashmir as well as on the mainland. The new strategy was said to have received a discreet nod from the USA which seemed to be still deluding herself by believing that the LeT, Jaish etc. were trained and tuned for "Kashmir Specific Jihad." The truth was otherwise. In the *madarsas* and training centres the peddlers of Jihad clearly identified the enemies of Islam as infidels-Jews (Israel), Christians (USA/Europe) and Hindus (India), strictly in that order. The sooner the US administration recognised that there were not and indeed could not be any India-specific Mujahids amongst those brainwashed to enforce their peculiar version of Nizam-e-Mustafa worldwide-repeat worldwide-the better for their well being.

As far as the fresh plans of terrorist attacks being planned by terrorist groups in Pakistan to which the PM had alluded to, some kind of sobriety and balance was visible in the diplomatic responses. After off the cuff irresponsible reaction by Pak MoS for external affairs, the emphasis was now upon sharing of the "credible information", the PM had spoken about. Obviously, the Indian government will take a view in the matter but the prevailing trust deficit between the two countries and the involvement of a faction of ISI, in the mischief was likely to stone wall sharing of such sensitive intelligence.

The public exposure of the Pakistan based terror groups' evil designs by the Prime Minister should be welcomed. It may also be safely assumed that the concerned government agencies had got down to the tasks cut out for them. But is that enough. Here was a war without borders in which no territory was to be occupied, nor any flags hoisted on captured forts. In fact, the entire nation of 100 crores plus and its numerous vital assets spread all over the enormous land mass and high seas were on the enemy's radar. Could such a non-conventional war respecting no rules honouring, no conventions could be won without people's awareness, mobilisation and indeed their participation? If not, did the government have any road map of people's role in fighting and winning this war? It should be remembered that the threat from Pakistan was no passing irritant but a long term, determined and meticulously planned 'Jihad' backed by almost inexhaustible manpower, financial resources and military and technology hardware.

The operations by LeT, Jaish and others of their ilk supported by indigenous terror cells like SIMI, Indian Mujahideen and Taliban-e-Hind had the capacity to indulge in subversion and sabotage at a somewhat large scale encompassing a vast and wide spread target zone. This posed a serious threat to the peace and progress of this country. The harsh reality can be ignored only at the peril of national security. Comprehensive, innovative and effective counter measures should urgently be engineered to stop the enemy in its track sand neutralise it if it managed to sneak in. Coming days, months and perhaps years could really be tough. Is the nation being prepared for this?

Pakistan: Internal Chaos and International Isolation

Ali Sarwar Naqvi, a former Pakistan diplomat in his perceptive piece titled "International Isolation" *Dawn* (August 17, 2011) wrote, "As has happened several times in the past, Pakistan is facing international isolation once again. Somehow we land ourselves in a situation ever so often where we are on one side and the rest of the world is on the other". Interestingly, he quotes four instances from history to illustrate his point. Two of these directly concern India.

First, "military action in the then East Pakistan when we thought we were right and the rest of the world thought that we were wrong."

Second, "our military adventure in Kargil, which was considered by the rest of the world as irresponsible and likely to provoke war."

Third, "the execution of an elected prime minister, deposed by extra-constitutional action. Again the world appealed to our leadership not to take the dire step, but we did."

Fourth, "the recognition of the Taliban regime in Afghanistan; when the rest of the world, except for two countries, shunned it, we recognised it."

"The result in each episode", he wrote, "was international isolation, which took us a long time to get out of."

"The terrorism and violence emanating from Pakistani territory seems to be the proverbial last straw. Many terrorist incidents, starting with the London underground attack and the infamous Mumbai attacks in 2008 among others, were found to have a Pakistani connection, or suspected of one. We have become the prime exporter of terrorism abroad, as well as its hapless victims at home...As a result, no country worth the name now wishes to do business with us, allow our students, or our professionals and academics, or our visitors and tourists to enter its territory. Likewise, outsiders avoid coming to Pakistan." "No wonder", he wrote "we are facing international isolation, and one which is far worse than we have ever experienced that may break the camel's back."

"It is just not the United States" "he emphasised", that harbours a negative perception about us, it is almost the whole world that is becoming wary of us." According to him, "the solution, though appearing difficult at first sight, is also very simple. We can put aside the other problems for the time being and concentrate on only one for the moment — the elimination and eradication of terrorism — to overcome this debilitating isolation". Ali Sarwar Naqvi is not the only one in Pakistan to see the writing on the wall, rationally analyse the situation and come up with honest and practical responses to the ugly situation.

In fact, the Islamic republic of Pakistan was tottering on the edge of a terrible precipice. The nation was torn down the middle by sectarian conflict. Its polity, establishment, defence forces and society were fractured and deeply penetrated by the extreme Islamist zealots. A gasping economy was barely breathing on the oxygen provided by the US aid. The Pakistan decision to invoke sovereignty rather than express satisfaction at the elimination of Osama bin Laden, the foremost leader of international terrorism in the successful clandestine operation in Abbotabad placed so much strain on the already soured US-Pak relations that the later could exercise the option of terminating economic aid. The signs for Pakistan were ominous.

Pakistans' duplicity in respect of domestic and international terrorism has been completely exposed. The international community has arrived at the conclusion that Pakistan not only tolerates, but promotes and exports terrorists and armed marauders to run riot all over the world She allows them safe havens, provides space and facilities for running training camps. Pakistan was thus perceived as the epicentre of international terrorism and the most dangerous place in the world.

The problem in reality is with the Pakistan Army, who back seat drive the state bandwagon. They are averse to eliminate or even disband the so called "home grown terrorism", promoted and preserved as strategic assets against India. The truth is that Pakistan's problems across the board were the product of the totally insane perception that India was out to destroy that country and should, therefore, be treated as enemy number one. It, however, seems that, more and more thinking people and more importantly the common citizens of that country were seeing through the game of the Pakistan army to use India card as the red herring to retain their grip on the country's power structure. There were also indications that an influential section of Pakistan defence establishment was tending to recognise the senselessness and stupidity of perpetual hate India stance at the cost of Pakistan's economic and political interests. More over, the speed with which Tehrik-e-Taliban, Pakistan and their collaborators were extending their reach and terror to all the nooks and corners of the country, there was not much time and not many options left with those who wish to save their country from the danger of extreme Islamist takeover. Let there be no doubt in anybody's mind that undue delay in establishing control in Pakistan which placed Pakistan's nuclear assets within reach of the terrorists would definitely invite swift and decisive international intervention without any concern for sovereignty of a country turning rouge. The stakes for the world community in the case were too high to brook such niceties.

Indo-Pak Relations

War Mongering and Peace Process can't Go Together

Hafiz Saeed, the patron of dreaded terrorist organisation Lashkar-e-Toiba and Jammat-ud-Dawa supremo, branded by the United Nations Security Council as a terrorist was apparently fielded by a frustrated Pakistan establishment to lambast India on the twin issues of Kashmir and the water dispute that formed the sheet anchor of Pakistan position during the recent Indo-Pak foreign Secretary level conference in New Delhi. This appeared to be Pakistan's bloody minded response of the Indian insistence on action against the Hafiz for his role in 26/11 Mumbai terror strikes. Significantly, Prime Minister Gillani of Pakistan had only the other day added the water dispute to the Indo-Pak negotiation menu and placed it at par with Kashmir.

In an interview on the frontline programme of Pakistani *Express News Channel*, his first appearance after he was put under "house arrest" in the wake of Mumbai terror attack, Saeed said, "Look at India's attitude especially after the 9/11 attack. It has taken advantage of Pakistan's weakness and made dams and stopped our water". Please check your fact first. For record, no dams were constructed in Jammu & Kashmir after 9/11 and the water was flowing down from our sources as usual. Remember, it is our water that we share with Pakistan under a treaty after signing which the then Prime Minister Nehru said that he had paid a very heavy price for peace with Pakistan. Pakistan continued to exact the price but what about the ever elusive peace? The Hafiz further declared, "Pakistan for (on the pretext) its defence, will have to fight a war at all costs with India if it is not prepared to talk on Kashmir and water". "If India doesn't hold talks and is not willing to accept the problems over the water what other option (except war) is left?" he demanded; and declared, "If there is a war between Pakistan and India, the Pakistan army, people and JUD will stand united and fight with India". Imagine, JUD, a proclaimed charity fighting a war against the third largest army in the world. Or has the time to shed the pretence has arrived? In any case the nexus between the Pakistan civil and military establishment and the Lashkar was now out into the open. It may be recalled that Hafiz Saeed was an honoured guest in an *Iftar* party hosted by a corps commander in his headquarters' officers' mess during the last holy month of fasting the Ramadan.

War was also on the mind of the Pakistan army chief Gen. Kiyani when he suddenly and without any provocation dug up the "Cold Start Military doctrine of India" for comments. He boasted that his army was ready to give a befitting reply to any attack from the eastern front. But where was the threat from India? So was he hallucinating, or was something really cooking?

The world knows that India is and has been a victim of Pakistan aggressive and subversive designs ever since its creation. All these six decades plus, India has exercised tremendous restraint and reacted only when it became inevitable and that too in a measured manner. Her magnanimity in repatriating 93 thousand prisoners of war in 1972 and vacating huge chunks of territory occupied after fierce fighting was a part of history. We know fully well that Pakistan and her Pan-Islamic mentors had set on the path of not only pursing the strategy of "bleeding India with thousand cuts." but also to cause its Balkanisation. Our Prime Minister repeatedly asserts that there was no alternative to Dialogue between the neighbours. Having said this, when faced with decades old proxy war and renewed threats of war, India must not only keep its powder dry but also let it be known that its decency should not be mistaken for weakness. It also needed to be forcefully stated that the nuclearisation of the two countries did not confer any special advantage upon Pakistan. The nuclear balance should in fact act as a deterrent against any military adventurism. The history of cold war at its peak when numerous nuclear weapons were poised for launch, testified to this reality.

Earlier the foreign Secretary level Indo-Pak talks in New Delhi had begun on an ominous note. India pressed for evidence of concrete and convincing action against the perpetrators of the Mumbai carnage for which credible evidence had been provided. Special emphasis was laid on action against Hafiz Saeed, the Patron of Lashkar-e-Toiba, the premier terrorist outfit with international reach. Pakistan, on the other hand, harped on the resumption of composite dialogue to resolve "core issues of Kashmir and water dispute" sidestepping the stated Indian concerns. As the Indian side solidly stood its ground, there was no meeting ground at all. Neither party was left with any space for manoeuvre. No wonder the laboriously managed contact ended as it did.

The Pakistan delegation went home declaring that their country was not interested in off and on contacts conveying not so subtly that any future talks will have to be on their terms. Indian position was that Pakistan must first prove her *bona fides* in implementing the undertaking that her soil will not be used for terrorist attacks against India and tender proof of effective action taken against those involved in 26/11 Mumbai attack the focus being on action against Hafiz Saeed, the Lashkar patron.

During his last Washington visit Prime Minister Manmohan Singh had made pointed mention of two elements as prerequisite to the resumption of the composite dialogue with Pakistan. One, effective action against the culprits of 26/11 Mumbai terror assault. Two, the dismantling of the terrorist training infrastructure in Pakistan. It was, therefore, only logical for the Indian side to press for Pakistan response on both these elements. As a matter of fact, the issue of dismantling terrorist training infrastructure was fundamental to the termination of cross-border terrorism. Moreover, any action in this behalf was both quantifiable and verifiable. According to Defence Minister Anthony the number of terrorist training camps in Pakistan stood at 42 on the last count. Amongst these, the Mansehra terrorist training facility in Pakistan was rated by many experts as "world class". Obviously, no meaningful negotiations could be conceived without the demolition of the terror infrastructure existing in Pakistan.

As a responsible nuclear power India had unilaterally announced the policy of 'no first use' of nuclear weapons. But it should not be taken to mean that we were either lowering our guards, or our defence forces would fail, or falter in any manner if a war was forced upon us. We seek peace and as the Prime Minister said we were willing to walk an extra mile if Pakistan effectively acts against terrorism. The people of Pakistan in general and the civil society in particular must rise to the occasion and cry a halt to this insane war mongering particularly at a time when that country was itself bleeding from persistent and diabolical assaults by the fundamentalist terrorist. Geography, ethnicity, history, culture and tradition dictated peace and friendship between the two neighbours. Peace in the region was indeed a necessity not a luxury. Surely peace can not be built on the dubious foundation of insincerity, duplicity and brinkmanship. Bluff and bluster have time and again proved not only ineffective but also counter-productive. The sooner the rulers of Pakistan wake up to the realities the better for the two neighbours as well as for the entire South Asia.

Pakistan: A Rogue State Sliding into Anarchy

The outgoing US Chief of Joint Staff Admiral Mullen did his country and the world community a signal service by comprehensively exposing the Pak ISI-Haqqani network nexus and pointedly accusing the agency of connivance with the Haqqani in the recent attack on US embassy in Kabul. In an unprecedented condemnation, he described the Haqqani network as the "veritable arm" of Pakistan's Inter-Services Intelligence (ISI). "If they keep killing our troops, that would not be something we would just sit idly by and watch," Mullen warned. Earlier, US ambassador Cameron Munter told Radio Pakistan, "There is evident linking of the Haqqani network to the Pakistan government. This is something that must stop." These frontal assaults ripped apart the fig leaf of Pak pretence of partnership in the fight against international terrorism.

Resort to fake indignation and putting up a brave front impressed no one, not even ruling partymen. Pakistan's woes further multiplied and panic spread in the corridors of power in Islamabad as a resolution to halt critical military and economic US aid was introduced in the US congress. It was in this backdrop that General Kiyani and his ISI boys contrived the all parties conference with the twin aims of obtaining endorsement of its handling of the security situation within Pakistan and initiatives in Afghanistan. and putting up a strong show of national solidarity. Prime Minister Gilani was happy to go along as long as his job was secure.

The all parties conference called by the government of Pakistan met behind closed doors on 20th September last. Predictably, it unanimously adopted the resolution calling for a chance for peace "as military action had failed to produce the desired results in a decade old war waged by the US coalition in Afghanistan and the Pak army operations in Waziristan". The message being, "Silence guns and get on with negotiations with the Taliban - both of the Afghan and Pakistan varieties with an open mind to accommodate the terrorists". The fiasco in Afghanistan, according to conference sources could certainly not be attributed to the alleged support by certain sections of the Pakistan Army to "Afghan terrorist groups". Actually, the High Command of war weary Pakistan army was under tremendous internal pressures from its middle wrung of its own leadership demanding a halt to "war with its own people" and a soft approach towards Islamist militants. The APC rubbished all such allegations and gave the Pakistan army and the ISI a clean chit. Task one accomplished.

The sources also revealed that the conference mulled over policy course correction with the aim of restoring. "Pakistan's compromised self-respect". It claimed consensus amongst the leaders to discard the current dependence on loans advanced by international lending institutions or foreign aid, which never come without strings attached and strive to work for economic self-reliance. "Trade, not aid," was expounded as the new mantra. The politicians, the leaks gave out, dutifully pledged to stand behind the government and the armed forces, should it come to dealing with any military threat posed to the country from any quarter. Task two also accomplished. Sadly, the façade of unity and unanimity did not last long.

The fistcrack showed when reports of a caustic query by Nawaz Shrief as to "why no one in the whole world believed our assertion that Pakistan was not aiding the anti-US forces in Afghanistan." According to him, there had to be, *daal mein kuch kaala*. Interestingly, *Achakzai* reportedly commented that if the ISI chief wanted there would be peace in Afghanistan within a month's time.

The APC resolve to set up a parliamentary committee to oversee and monitor developments on a monthly basis to ensure that its recommendations reflect in government policy provoked adverse reaction in the media. "Clearly, this mechanism suits the power troika, the president, the prime minister and the army chief. The first two do not wish to annoy the last mentioned by taking foreign policy and national security debate to the open and constitutionally empowered institution that is parliament." Wrote an eminent columnist in *Dawn*, "But unless we get there, and discuss and debate at length critical issues like redefining national and foreign policies and do so in a democratically transparent manner, we will not be taken seriously by the world no matter how many APCs we convene and how many consensuses we achieve under duress behind closed doors, he concluded.

A frustrated opposition finally decided to come clean on the reality of the all-parties conference. "The biggest casualty in the briefing given to the September 29 all parties conference (APC) by Inter-Services Intelligence (ISI) Director General Lt. Gen. Ahmed Shuja Pasha was the 'so-called US threat' to Pakistan", the leader of the Opposition in the National Assembly Chaudhry Nisar Ali Khan told *The News*. The Foreign Minister Hina Rabbani Kharhe said, "didn't inform the audience whether or not there is really a US threat; whether or not it is imminent, and if it is imminent what are the options available to Pakistan." Ch. Nisar's discloser that "Gen. Pasha's briefing was very brief and it spanned just about eight minutes, revolving on a one-point agenda — clarifying the spy agency's position on the Haqqani Network, took the cake.

Addressing his party's newly elected working committee members, Sharif reminded them that he always considered President Zardari a 'threat' for democracy which he claimed proved to be true. He accused the government of manipulating members of the parliament to get resolutions passed. "The present government had given the people of Pakistan nothing but humiliation," and looking at the present state of Pakistan was heartbreaking." The battle lines were drawn.

In response to the scathing criticism by the main Opposition in the national assembly, Prime Minister Yusuf Raza Geelani has dared Mian Nawaz Shareif to move a no-confidence motion against his government. He threw the gauntlet after getting MQM back on board and mending fences with Ch. Shujahat Hussain and his PML-Q. Pakistan could certainly not afford in fighting at a time when international marginalisation, inter necine conflicts, economic chaos and the dubious distinction of being branded as a rogue state has made Pakistan a laughing stock in the world community.

The collapse of the unity façade so painstakingly put together by the ISI even before the ink had dried on the resolutions passed by the all parties conference signals the diminishing clout of the Pakistan army high command. It also provides credence to NSA Menon's perception that Pakistan "was sliding into anarchy and multiple extra-constitutional elements were fiddling with levers of power". Now come the Memogate controversy, the conflicting positions taken there upon by the government and the Pakistan chief of Staff, General Kiyani and ISI chief General Pasha, the sudden departure of President Zardari to Dubai on the pretext of ill health, his sudden return and the on-going PIL in that country's Supreme Court conspicuously flag serious contours of crisis facing Pakistan.

The unprecedented crisis in our immediate neighbourhood with a real threat of take over by Pan-Islamic extremists, or their fellow travellers looming on the horizon is obviously of grave concern for us in India. Such a development would enable Islamist terrorists to gain access to the Pak nuclear arsenal creating a terrible situation for the entire mankind. Such is the writing on the wall. The civilised world, particularly India, have to hammer out an adequate and timely response to the grave threat to world peace. Contingency plans should be update and pre-emptive operational mechanism primed. This must be supplemented by speedy reach out to the democratic, secular segments within the socio-political and defence establishment of Pakistan. The aim should be to pledge and provide all necessary support to enable them to take on the extremists head on. As of today, the violent, well organised and fully armed noisy minority has succeeded in frightening and silencing the vast majority of decent, peace loving and moderate people of Pakistan. The saner elements are however, not about to give up. If moral, diplomatic and material support were forthcoming from international community they can certainly turn the tables, rescue Pakistan and provide big boost to moderate democratic Islamic forces trying to assert in different parts of the world. The billion dollar question is, will the world community act and act in time?

10

Pakistan Under Threat

Trouble in Balochistan

Is Pakistan Heading for Another Split?

Balochistan, the geo-strategically sensitive and mineral rich province of the Islamic Republic of Pakistan (347,641 sq. km.) encompassing 43 per cent of that country's total land mass and 75 per cent of its coast line is enmeshed in the latest version of the Great Game. Bounded by Afghanistan on the north-west, Iran on the west and Arabian sea on the south it is a principal trade route between south-west Asia, Central Asia and South Asia. Ironically, Pakistan's current patron, the Unite States of America is the leading player in the game aimed at destabilising Pakistan and carving out an independent state of Balochistan.

Historically, Balochistan offers an excellent opportunity to bolster the Great Game. Baloch people never really accepted the parceling of their land by British Indian government, Iran and Afganistan amongst themselves in the nineteenth century to thwart the expansionist designs of Russia. The Bloach have since been yearning for reunification of their country and the people. Even more than unity of the people, it is a question of their dignity and their tribal pride.

Official circles in Islamabad are reported to be quite open in accusing, Iran, some Gulf countries and the United States of promoting Bloch partisans. The US move is also seen in the context of her plans to "redraw the map of the Muslim world in the middle east and south-west Asia being referred to as "broader middle east". "Break up of larger Muslim states, redrawing borders between some of them, creating new political entities–all these are part of the new strategic game plan (of United States), says Shirin Mazari. AH Amin, the author of' Pakistan Army, is more specific about the American intentions in the region. "The new US strategy," he says, "is possibly the creation of a Kurd state. If it is extended to creation of a new Bloch state, it should not be a surprise." "An independent Blochistan state", he says, "would give the US an excellent base which could possibly replace both Afghanistan and Pakistan to strike at future strategic targets in Central Asia, Middle East and East China." Balochistan is also rated as one of the few Muslim areas with least anti-American sentiment and minimum influence of 'Islamists'.

Gwadar, the deep-sea port of tremendous importance from the economic as well as the strategic point of view is in the eye of the storm. It was identified by Pakistan in 1964 and handed over for development to China in 2001. The appearance of the United States in Afghanistan in the same year resulted in acceleration of work on the project, an estimated 80 per cent of the funding being provided by China. The involvement of China as the dominant partner in developing and controlling this gateway that when operationalised will be the center of trade with energy rich Gulf countries, central Asian Republics, China, Afghanistan, and Iran has understandably caused serious concerns in the USA, Iran, Russia, Britain, some Gulf countries and India. India, in addition, has security concerns as Gwadar will provide Pakistan Navy strategic depth vis-a-vis India along the coast line. The ensuing complex geo-political game has placed the Bloch population in Pakistan, Iran and Afghanistan at the center of the international concerns further fueling the quest for an independent Balochistan.

Internally, the chips are stacked against Pakistan. The vast landscape of Balochistan is mostly barren and rugged, only

5 per cent of which is arable. It is home to just about 5 per cent of Pakistan's population that has a predominantly tribal social structure rooted in kinship and fierce loyalty to the hereditary Sardars. Its low density of population, internationally recognised but largely untapped rich mineral resources and huge gas deposits provide an irresistible pull for exploiters and settlers.

The Pakistani rulers, uncomfortable with freedom loving tribals and their stubbornly independent Sardars have since the very inception of that country promoted a change in the demographic character of Balochistan through migration from other provinces particularly, Punjab and Sindh. Balochistan, which became a province of Pakistan in 1970 with the merger of Quetta and Kalat divisions was kept under central rule until the first provincial elections in 1972.

The people of Balochistan have been waging a guerilla war ever since the dawn of independence in 1947. Three major armed conflicts ensued in 1948,1958 and 1973. The last two were primarily reactions to the demographic changes unleashed by Pakistan governments in pursuance of their policy of colonisation. The worst confrontation in 1973 was triggered by the tribal attack on Goth Mohammad Husain in Pat Feeder area of the Katch district, a Punjabi settlement on December, 1972. Already unnerved by the loss of East Pakistan, the Bhutto government responded with fierce and unprecedented brutality. In a no holds barred military operation involving about eighty thousand troops, all the superior fire power of the Pakistan defence forces including its Air Force, 5,300 Baloch guerrillas and 3,300 Pakistani soldiers are estimated to have perished. And yet it took more than four years for the situation to be brought under control. Two most prominent leaders of the revolt Sardar Atta Ullah Mengal (the first Baloch chief minister in the NAP-Jui coalition government) and Khair Bux Mari went into self-exile. The embers of revolt were, however, kept burning by the Baloch youth under the leadership of Nawab Akbar Bugti. The anger against oppression and discrimination sporadically erupted in violence, the only means of expression of dissent known to the warrior Baloch tribes. There were 15 bomb blasts in Quetta between June and December, 2003.

The eclipse of the Taliban in the neighbouring Afghanistan and the radical transformation of the world scene post-9/11 seriously and comprehensively impacted the geo-politically sensitive Balochistan. Recognising the need to assuage the hurt feelings of the Balochis and buy peace, President Musharraf even went to the extent of tendering apology to the people of Balochistan. In a speech at Quetta on 6th October, 2003 he said;

"Blochistan did not get a fair treatment in the past. It was denied its due rights, funds and resources. Some people in the past committed excesses on the people of Balochistan...I apologise for the excesses perpetrated on the people of Balochistan."

Apparently the apology was cosmetic and tactical. The harsh and arrogant reaction richly laced with threats to the outbreak of the last March violence by the very same General Musharraf proves this beyond doubt. On the political front, Musharraf ingeniously managed to nearly exclude the restive and defiant regional parties through the decree prescribing graduation as the minimum qualification for contesting the elections. The exclusion from electoral contest and the consequent denial of opportunity to control the state apparatus further heightened the alienation and frustration of the tribals. The fires of revolt were stoked by the fear of demographic changes particularly through the influx of the 'hated Punjabis' and the Afghan refugees following the fall of the Taliban.

The trouble brewing in Balochistan erupted into a bloody clash between the tribal militants and the Pakistan army in the town of Dera Bugti in the second week of March 2011. The militants attack on country's largest gas field Sui in January 2011 left at least fifteen people dead. In the Thursday, 17th clash, eight Pak soldiers were killed and 23 others wounded.

Nawab Bugti, whose men were reported to have encircled 300 Pak soldiers told a government sponsored parliamentary delegation that, "we have at least 62 dead. There were 32 Hindus mostly women and children (killed).

"In the temple, one mother with her two children and another woman with her niece were killed, their bodies completely shattered", he added. He also alleged that the "government forces used machine guns and helicopter gun ships. They fired all weapons that the army has except nuclear devices. But, I presume, if need be, nobody will give a second thought about using them (the nukes) to exterminate the Baloch." Brigadier Salim Nawaz, the commander of para military troops in the region showed to the delegation video images of heavily armed tribesmen ringing the fort. Brig. Nawaz said that the tribal fighters were well supplied with sophisticated weapons but declined to name the source of supply. Officials said Nawab Bugti alone has a private army of about four thousand.

The reach of the current phase of revolt in Balochistan extends to neighboring Iran and Oman. The 'Seitan-Blochistan', the wild west of Iran, a heaven for dealers in lethal weapons and illicit drugs has emerged as the favourite sanctuary of Baloch militants. The wealthy Baloachs of Oman, where Baloch population outnumber native omanese, have been liberally financing the separatists. The chips are obviously getting stacked against Pakistan in Balochistan. Added to all this is the all pervading Baloach fear of Punjabi domination and declared determination to thwart their 'evil intentions'. Sardar Akbar Mengal, leader of Baloch National Party (BNP) gave expression to this sentiment when he declared in the provincial assembly in October, 2003:

"We will not allow settlement of unrestricted Punjabis in Gwadar even at the cost of our lives. The people of Blochistan will never forgive them (Punjabis) as they are engaged in sell out of our motherland to appease their masters. If government persists with its plan of protecting Punjabis, then the country will have to face dismemberment." *(Pak Tribune,* October 6, 2003). Indian interest in the playing out of the Great Game in Balochistan in months and years to come is deep and abiding. The crucial question, however, is: how will it impact on the integrity of Pakistan?

The Cult of Taliban

History is witness to the conception and promotion of the anti-Soviet Jehad in Afghanistan by the USA and Pakistan. In 1980s, the CIA forged the jihad and jihadis in collaboration with the Pak ISI to serve the vested interest to evict Soviets from Afghanistan. It was the most cost-effective option for USA to fight the war so far away from its soil. "Bands of Jihadi boys were brainwashed, nurtured and trained at the behest of the Americans with petro-dollars flowing in from Arabia to carry out lethal missions against the Soviets in Afghanistan in the 1980s. Today they had grown up to be terror machines, churning out young frustrated clones to take on their masters' mentors." Remember American President Ronald Reagan's photo session with Afghan warlords in the Oval Office. It speaks volumes.

The war in Afghanistan resulted in a two way movement. Lakhs of refugees fled their homeland to safety in Pakistan, and thousands of Pashtuns crossed the Durrand Line, the other way to fight alongside their clansmen. The complexion of the conflict radically changed when the Soviets departed from Afganistan leaving the governance of the country in the hands of Najibullah and his communist party. Mislead into seeking asylum in the United Nations HQs in Kabul, Najibullah was dragged out and hanged in public. The Mujahideen had a clear field and quickly set upon each other to grab the throne in Kabul. Fed up with the feuding factions of Mujahideen, their rampant corruption and galloping slide down in popular acceptability, the US-UK-PAK Axis forged the Taliban, primarily consisting of Pushtun students reared in *madarsas* and steeped in Islamic extremism. The *madarsas* in Pakistan were converted into recruitment factories for the new breed of Mujahideen, who came to be named as the Taliban.

The battle for ascendency brought the Taliban led by Mullah Umar and the Northern Alliance of the Lion of Panchsher, Commander Ahmad Shah Masood in headlong armed collision. An allout ethnic war erupted. Thousands of Pakistani Pashtuns rushed to Afghanistan to join the ranks of their Afghan counterparts. This, however failed to change the course of the conflict. The Afghan Taliban retreated to Pakistan in 2001 after suffering reverses. The Pakistani Taliban played hosts to their uprooted brethren for which they were stated to have been handsomely rewarded. The sources of supply, the mode and the rationale of the transfer of the funds, the military and communication equipment were shrouded in mystery. The finger of suspicion at times pointed towards some Gulf countries who were known to acquire sophisticated military hardware far in excess of their actual requirements and even place orders for those items which were not part of the equipment of their own Armed forces. Did it also have something to do with joint enterprise in Drug trafficking ? These and other questions beg answers. But neither the CIA, nor the Pak ISI were about to disclose what obviously was within their knowledge.

Within Pakistan the plan worked smoothly until post-9/11 US attack on Afghanistan which changed the entire context. As Musharraf dumped the Afghan Taliban and jumped on the US-led international anti-terror coalition, the ideologically motivated Jehadi elements who otherwise might have taken a bit longer to usurp Pakistani society's breathing space, felt compelled to move out of the shadows. Flush with funds, weaponry and fundamentalist motivation, the Pakistani Taliban grew in number and influence, especially between and 2001 to 2004. The patronage of the Pakistan government albeit from behind the scene, and support the ISI provided made their task much easier. In half-hearted army actions, local police, the frontier scouts and the assorted army units were humbled.The drama of captures and exchanges for the extremists held in custody by Pakistan/NWFP governments further enhanced their prestige and clout. A weak and vacillating Pakistan whose establishment was infiltrated by the Taliban, thus boosted morale and enhanced their capability. Number of high profile terrorist strikes across the country notably in capital Islamabad and cultural capital Lahore frightened the weak kneed and prompted the national assembly into surrender. The promulgation of Nizam-e-Adil Regulation marked the high point in their march towards total control of Swat and the Malkand Division which comprised of one third of the NWFP. The leadership of the Taliban through their consistent acts of making and breaking deals, unleashing waves after waves of terror, brutal, barbaric and indiscriminate assassination, spate of suicide bombings and by debunking the very concept of a nation state of Pakistan have declared their intentions. They aimed to establish a Taliban 'emirate', or state in Fata. The expansion of that particular concept of statehood translated by the fundamentalist into their peculiar version of Nizam-e-Mohammadi to embrace the whole of Pakistan was being witnessed today. Let there be no doubt that the Pakistan Taliban were out to take over the whole of Pakistan with its nuclear assets which if media reports were to be believed "would be used to destroy USA".

So what exactly were the contours of kind of Nizam, the Taloban aimed to establish, to begin within Swat and eventually in entire Pakistan? Maulana Sufi Mohd., the Tehrik Nifaz Nizam-e-Mohammadi chief, had emerged as the key figure in this context. The Swat Taliban had declared time and again that they would abide by the concept of Sharia and Nizam-e-Adl that is acceptable to Sufi Mohammad. The Sufi (only in name) possessed no credentials of an Islamic scholar. Neither he pretended to be one. But at the same time he considered himself competent to freely comment on topics that impact daily life of the citizens and the functions of the state. Interestingly, Tehrik Nifaz Nizam-e-Mohammadi was outlawed by Gen. Musharraf on Jan. 12, 2002, Maulana Sufi Mohammad was, in fact, sentenced on April 24, 2002 to 10 years' imprisonment for inciting people to cross over into Afghanistan and fight US forces. The Maulana enjoys full support of son-in-law, Fazlullah, who heads the Taliban in Swat. A meglomininae and psychopath he had played havoc with the lives of a hapless population and forcibly enforced his writ in the valley. Mufti Mohd. also enjoyed cosy relationship with Baiuulh Mehsood, a more vicious version of Fazlullah.

Anees Jillani of the *News* interviewed Sufi Mohd. in October 1994. Even at that point of time, he expressed his anti-democracy views unambiguously and with the same vigour that he was doing nowadays. "For him, the judiciary then was 'English law' and, therefore, un-Islamic and unacceptable. His concept of Sharia then and now is a simple judicial system in which judges, or *qazis* as he referred to them, would preside over courts and dispense quick and affordable justice. The chosen *qazis* were to match the specifications set forth by him both in terms of character and physical features, meaning they had to be pious and bearded. "The top cleric of the TNSM repeated his views in a huge public rally in Mingora after the collapse of the Nizam-e-Adil deal. He again pronounced democracy to be un-Islamic and declared that the High Courts and the Supreme Court consisted of non-believers, and added that only those who know Sharia could be appointed as judges. He said that "the verdicts of the Swat Sharia courts could not be challenged in High Courts, or in the Supreme Court". The entire world is aware of the shocking public flogging of women and barbaric beheading of persons who had no access to any kind of civilised judicial system. The demolition of schools especially the Girl's schools, bombing of *Ziarats* and *Mazara* held in reverence by the vast majority of Muslims in Pakistan and assassination of revered *Pirs* and *Faqirs* had produced a highly volatile reaction creating an environment ideal for the making of a civil war.

On his visit to the area prior to the launching of *ops rah-i-Nijat* by the army, Jillani reported that "there is hardly any police station, or check post left in the valley. Almost all major buildings stand destroyed, or damaged. And as one steps outside

Mingora, particularly in the small town of Kanju, every second house is scarred by gunshots. The most depressing aspect, however, is the systematic destruction of schools—more than 200 are said to have been destroyed—and this is not confined to girl's schools. A few tent schools have been set up at some locations but a vast majority of children have nowhere to go. All key hospitals have been ransacked by militants—everything from beds to medicines have been taken away to furnish healthcare facilities for their compatriots". In the neighbouring district of Buner, private property had been seized and plundered, the youth were being both pressurised and enticed to join the Taliban ranks. The imposition of *Jazia* on the local sikhs, the forcible seizure of their properties and virtual expulsion of the community from their homes of centuries had already pricked the conscience of the world community on the arbitrary, atrocious and abominable Taliban decreed punishments. According to Columnist Shafi Kamran, "The entire judicial system thus is reduced to the application 'Hadood' punishments: floggings, beatings and amputations. Thus the *qazi,* arguably the most important functionary in justice provision, is nearly always invisible, while the crowd, the victim and those meting out a punishment play a central role. Justice is redefined as a means to subjugate and punish, with the entire collective crowd partaking in its....enactment", "doing away with hundreds of years of jurisprudence of classical Islamic law, of administrative procedures and methods of reasoning, of sources of law and juristic analysis, the Taliban have redefined Sharia as a performative tableau rather than a jurisprudential exercise" he concluded.

Exasperated, Cyril Almeida in article entitled "Cowering before the Taliban" published in the daily *Dawn* of 17 April, 2011 demanded, "Can no one in this country stand up and say this: we do not want to live in a society where a man, woman, or animal is flogged, where anyone's limb is hacked off, where anyone is stoned. And added, "We do not want to live in a society where such punishments have the sanction of the state. How did we get to this point where it is so difficult for anyone to just say that, and only that? Without qualifications, without apologies, without lowering his voice?" Yes, there were people courageous enough to speak out. The collective conscience of Pakistan had been aroused. Voices condemning the atrocities and challenging their perpetrators were being heard loud and clear. People from across the board, the *Barelvi* clerics whose view hold sway over vast majority of Muslims in Pakistan, the powerful army, tribal *Jirgas*, who had formed Lashkars fighting Taliban, intellectuals, prominent members of the civil society and above all the man in the street were speaking out. The bombing of civilian targets the assassination of the prominent and eminent public figures were instead of creating terror, unleashing a hurricane of anger and abhorrence that may drown the Taliban, and the un-Islamic and indeed inhuman cult that they represent.

Rise of Taliban

Pakistan's Nationalism in Conflict with Pan-Islamism?

"Pakistan's immense military power, the stunning intellect of its bureaucrats and the long tradition of accommodation and pragmatism among its politicians have all got together, but still can't put humpty-dumpty back together again." Wrote Musharraf Zaidi in his spiece titled *Why are we losing war against terror?* "This humpty-dumpty of sporadic, but increasingly fortified violence from a global gang of cavemen," he went on, "has fallen off the Durand 'Wall' into Pakistan and all over the NWFP. Yet Pakistan seems unable to resist and control its influence." "How could...Pakistan be so singularly incompetent in dealing with the virus of cavemen whose mantra is neither Islamic, nor tribal? Beheading journalists, blowing up in the middle of markets, and inciting young children to a black-hole life?" he demands and asserts, "This appetite for mayhem and destruction would be unrecognisable to Maudoodi, to Hassan Al Banna, even, dare I say, to Sayyid Qutub – whose own rage was tremendous, but whose mastery over Quranic text would have made it impossible for him to endorse the barbarianism and insanity of a terror". Wise words which, however, tragically went unheard in the loud boom of bomb blasts, shrieking cries of the wounded and breast beating and heart renting wails of mothers, sisters and daughters, whose innocent-loved ones, bread-winners and future hopes were blown into the void.

And yet the Taliban terror-wave was surging ahead submerging new and vital areas of Pakistan in ever expanding pools of blood. The blasting of the one thousand kg. explosives laden truck-bomb, driven by a Fidayeen at the entrance to the Islamabad Marriot hotel on 20th September, 2008 killed 40 on spot including the Czech ambassador to Pakistan (death toll since gone to 53) and wounded over 150, is still very fresh in people's memory. This terrorist strike in the capital of the Islamic Republic of Pakistan was rated as one of the worst in country's history.

The explosion was set off by a suicide bomber close to the Pakistan prime minister's house, where all the leaders of government including the three service chiefs and the chairman of the Joint chiefs of staff were dining. President Zardari has claimed that he and other guests in the dinner hosted by the speaker of Pakistan national assembly were targets. Those targeted owe their lives to the brave, vigilant and dedicated security staff (all civilians) deployed at the security barrier to the hotel. They valiantly blocked the entry of the Dumper to the hotel putting their lives on the line. This created the buffer sufficient to place the prime ministers' house and the entire civil and military leadership feasting therein out of harm's way. Witnesses said security guards and their gate posts were buried under a mound of rubble. By their sacrifice, they saved the entire civil and defence leadership of Pakistan from being blown into oblivion.

In a midnight address to the nation on the black Saturday itself, a visibly shaken Pakistan President Asif Ali Zardari declared, "The government will continue to fight terrorism and extremism in all its forms and manifestations and such dastardly acts cannot dent the government's commitment to fight this menace". The million dollar question was if, how and when would this resolve be translated into real effective action?

According to Abdullah Riar, a former aide to Late Benazir Bhuttoo, "The Marriott is an icon. It's like the twin towers of Pakistan." He may be exaggerating but the fact remains that the Islamabad Marriott was attacked by militants at least twice in the past, including a suicide attack in January 2007 that killed a policeman. Another reason for the hotel becoming a favoured target of the terrorists was its substantial and semi-permanent occupancy by Americans, many of whom were suspected to be CIA operatives. Coming in the wake of bombing in Kabul, Afghanistan and the Serena Hotel earlier this year, another gathering spot for foreigners, the Marriott attack appeared to flash a strong, renewed loud and clear message not just to Pakistan but to Washington and other Pakistani allies as well. Signal received but how and when were they going to respond to it?

The terrorist reach was now fast extending far beyond the confines of Fata, Swat and Waziristan. NWFP Governor Owais Ghani has warned Punjab that militancy was gaining strength in its backyard. "Militants in the tribal areas of the NWFP have established firm networking (with *jihadi* groups) in southern Punjab and most fresh recruits for suicide attacks were coming from there. Militant leaders and commanders were also coming from Punjab. The militants field commander in Swat, too, was from Punjab," he claimed. He said that it would be a grievous and costly error to treat the terrorist challenge emanating from the tribal areas as the NWFP specific problem. "It will be ill-advised to think that the militancy will remain confined to the NWFP. Militants' activities have already shifted to the settled areas and Punjab and they have established strong links with south Punjab. It's a national issue, a question of survival for (entire) Pakistan", he asserted.

Fierce clashes between rival Shia and Sunni tribes in different parts of Kurram Agency have added another worrisome dimension to the conflict. For obvious reasons, it would be unrealistic to expect Iran to remain a mute spectator either to the persecution of Shias in the so-called settled areas of Pakistan, or now in Kurram agency and adjoining areas. According to reports 18 days long clashes upto 24 August, 2008 had cost 400 lives. The efforts of the Hangu peace *jirga,* led by District Nazim Haji Khan Afzal failed to broker a ceasefire. Six Sunni tribes - Para Chamkani, Masozai, Ali Sherzai, Zermusht, Mengal and Sunni Bangash withdrew on the pretext of discussing the ceasefire proposal with their people and then convey their point of view to the *jirga.*

Pakistan was created as the homeland for Muslims of the Indian sub-continent. Religion was the very basis of its existence. This was enshrined in the Constitution of the *Mumalkit-e-Khudad*, the Islamic Republic of Pakistan. The mantra of nationhood taught to every Pakistani child in the school had become the national epitome. On the other hand, the chain of *madrasas* which churn out armies of students each year nearly bypassed the Pakistani national narrative, but subjected the students to a heavy over-dose of the Islamic chronicle. The products of the *madrasas* were, therefore, driven by the larger Islamic concept which defined the whole Muslim people as one nation, the *Ummah*. In the process, the Pakistani nationalism was diluted and dwarfed by Pan-Islamism. The conflict between the Pakistani identity and that of an indivisible worldwide *Ummah* caricatured, to put it mildly a split nationalism in Pakistan. It is this fractured vision of nationalism which is tearing the nation and the country apart. Today Pakistan's divide encompasses not only ethnic entities, sectarian groupings but infests the country's Islamic fabric itself.

The on-going war on terrorism impacts the national identity crisis in two ways. Firstly, a large number of Pakistanis oppose the government's policy of aligning with the USA and its allies in what they perceive as the Christian war against Islam. Secondly, the ruling elite, who have committed Pakistan to the international anti-terror coalition, and the leadership of the security forces are consequently obliged to wage war against their own kin in the terrorist ranks. This creates a dilemma for an average Pakistani, whereas a Pakistani soldier felt no hesitation in shooting at an Indian, or an Afghan unmindful of religious denominations, he had serious mental reservation in fighting his own people in Swat, Bajaur, or Waziristan. The dilemma was particularly unbearable when he was required to kill those claiming to be Mujahids fighting for the sake of Islam. Remember, the Pakistan army itself is groomed as an Islamic force! And then there were nagging doubt (sometimes more than doubts) about the sincerity and commitment of sizeable and powerful segments of military hierarchy, especially the ISI, believed to still be working in cohorts with Taliban on both sides of the Durand.

As the time passed, the very concept of a nation-state constructed on the foundation of religion proved a mere mirage. But leaders mostly Military Dictators, who imposed themselves on the luckless nation refused to learn the lesson. Musharaaf, the last Dictator, did resort to some half-hearted course correction measures after he dumped the Afghanistan Taliban and jumped on the USA driven anti-terrorist bandwagon. His simultaneous patronising of Islamic fundamentalists at home and abroad with a view to fuel the terror in Jammu & Kashmir, however, placed him in the precarious position of simultaneously riding two boats with predictable consequences. His legacy - the economy in shambles, the polity fractured, social structure torn asunder by poisonous sectarianism and a power vacuum at the top where the grave responsibility for the custody and operation of the nuclear button resides-stares the nation in face. To add to the misfortunes of Pakistan at this critical juncture in its history, a strong coalition between PPP and ML(N) which ousted Musharraf came unstruck earlier than expected.

The creator of Pakistan, Quaid-e-Azam Mohd. Ali Jinnah himself recognised this reality in his inaugural speech on 14th of August, 1947 to the Pakistan Constituent Assembly. If any further proof was needed to establish that ethnicity not religion provided an enduring adhesive that kept a nation in tact and on the move, it was conclusively provided by the break up of Pakistan and creation of Bangladesh. But Jinnah's assorted successors skept on parroting the discarded theme. Their hypocritical adherence to the rule by Islamic edicts (translated by the fundamentalists into their peculiar version of Nizam-e-Mustpha) was accorded official recognition by Zia-ul-Haq, the "Mullah in Khaki." It was now being exploited by the Taliban with significant success. The deadly brew was not only creating operational chaos but also poisoning the minds and hearts of the people.

The cobwebs need to be cleared from minds and a positive religious and cultural inputs to hearts of the Muslims of Pakistan provided. The former dictator and retired General Musharraf had taken a good initiative by focussing on the *Sufi* vision and practices of Islam which predominate in the sub continent. He himself became the patron of the sufi Promotion Council and involved electronic media and cultural organisations in the campaign in a big way. This was the only available and viable counter to the fundamental extremism. The present dispensation will do well to carry forward the campaign in a more innovative and forceful manner. Once the people recognise the extremist interpretation of Islam as alien to their traditional beliefs and time honoured practices, they were bound to reject both the Taliban and fundamentalism. The realisation that they were fighting a home-grown terrorist minority holding the entire nation to ransom, and recklessly inflicting death and destruction in their quest to impose its will by force, must dawn before they can be mobilised to not only outrightly reject the Taliban but also massively participate in the war against terror. Therein lies the hope for the nation and the nation-state of Pakistan.

War against Taliban-What will it Take Pak Army to Win?

During his current visit to the United States, President Zardari of Pakistan was questioned about the imminent threat of the Taliban takeover of his country. Zardari instead of giving a direct answer posed a counter question, "with seven million strong Pakistan army how could this be possible"? The questioner left the matter at that point and moved on. President Zardari's counter-raised some pertinent questions, which need to be addressed in the interest of a realistic and authentic appraisal of the implication of meteoric rise of Taliban in Pakistan-a state perched precariously on the brink.

The Pakistan President had a long list of options from which to draw strength and support for his position. As the elected head of the state in a democratic country, he was expected to stress upon the rejection of the cult of Taliban by the vast majority of the people of Pakistan in the last elections. As it is, most Pakistanis who were adherents of Islamic *sufi* mysticism and venerated saints and their shrines dotted across the country considered the extremist savagery, brutal practices and senseless indiscriminate blood shedding abhorrent. It seems not only President Zardari and the US establishment but all other stake-holders: the establishment, the parliament, the civil society, the intelligentsia and even the non-fundamentalist clergy have chosen to bet on the Pak Army as the instrument for containing and eliminating the scourge of the Taliban. Given the conditions prevailing in Pakistan, there was little choice. The stakes of the nation-state of Pakistan and the civilised world in this confrontation were indeed very high. Obviously, the success, or failure of enterprise would primarily hingo on the character, state of health, commitment and capability of the army and its leadership.

The partition of the Indian sub-continent and creation of Pakistan in August 1947, brought about the division of the British Indian colonial army, a portion of which constituted the Pakistan Army. Sadly, it had not changed its colonial character even after sixty eight years of independence.

The paramount duty of the British Indian army was to ensure order within India and protect the interests of the *Raj* against the challenges of the 'revolutionary' elements. In exchange for the services rendered, the British empire, generously rewarded the officers and the men. They were favoured with the allotment of precious land, particularly in the newly irrigated parts of Punjab and Sindh. Much of the rank and file of the Pakistan Army hailed from Punjab and the NWFP-home to 'martial classes'.

The army was thus cast in the dual role of the patron state as well as its colonial strong arm appendage. After they became the masters of what they surveyed, the defence forces leadership spread their tentacles across the board—the civil administration, diplomacy, commerce and corporate sector. Corruption, nepotism and favouritism became the order of the day. In this new *avtar*, the army brass not only amassed undreamt of wealth but also simultaneously gathered huge amount of professional flab. This in turn significantly diluted its combat worthiness. Urgent correctives within the army structure and its interface with the other elements of the state apparatus were, therefore, absolutely necessary to correct, upgrade and enhance the capability of the Pak army to effectively take on the internationally supported fanatical Pakistani Taliban. As Ayjaz Amir appropriately put it, "The farce of senior commanders becoming real estate tycoons while still in service must end if we are to see the army function as a more effective fighting machine." Howsoever despite dilution of their combat capability, the Pak army officer corps remained close to the West in terms of personal life styles and ideological inclinations.

The smooth sailing boat was violently rocked during Gen. Zia-ul-Haq's stewardship of Pakistan. The Jehadi agenda furiously and uncompromisingly promoted by him 'polluted' the mindset, work culture and goals cherished by the nation's fighting machine. This imposed an element of severe and serious friction in the armed forces of Pakistan. With the passage of time the seedlings have flourished into deadly poisonous plants and vitiated the entire defence established. "It is not only the government but also the army that has the responsibility to clean up its act of setting a jihadi agenda back in Zia-ul-Haq's time," wrote Murtaza Razvi in the piece titled, 'When up against the militants', published in daily *Dawn*. "Bands of Jihadi boys were brainwashed, nurtured and trained at the behest of the Americans, with petro-dollars flowing in from Arabia to carry out lethal missions against the Soviets in Afghanistan in the 1980s. Today they have grown up to be terror machines, churning out young frustrated clones to take on their masters' mentors," he pointed out and pertinently asked, Who knows how many little bin Ladens and Al-Zawahiris they have in their fold, keeping liaisons with the intelligence and security apparatus, even as we speak? This could be an extreme view but the presence of Jehadi supporters and sympathisers in the defence ranks was a unpleasant reality. This dichotomy was at the core of the dilemma that griped the army leadership, especially at the middle level and debilitated its resolve to confront the Taliban resolutely.

The Pakistan army was calibrated and motivated to fight against India–the eternal enemy. "It hasn't a clue about fighting the Taliban in Swat and Waziristan. Indeed, the army's less than brilliant interventions in both these regions have been a powerful factor in making the Taliban more powerful", argued an eminent Pakistani security commentator, "To concentrate on the threat we face from within, the time may have come for us to give up on our India fixation. India is a headache. No doubt about it .....But a headache is one thing, an existential threat quite another."

President Zardari was on record having repeatedly stated that the never apprehended any threat from India. The comment of the ISI Chief Gen. Pasha some time back that "he was not stupid and knew that the threat to Pakistan came from the extremist and not India" becomes relevant in this context. Moving sixty thousand troops away from the Indian borders to the western front may be indicative of the beginning of a shift in strategic thinking in Pakistan. Some keen watchers of Indo-Pak-US triangle believe that the US had finally succeeded in convincing Pakistan that it faced no threat to its integrity from India. The question arises as to how real and enduring the shift is? The answer to this will impact not only the ability of Pakistan army to take its current anti-Taliban operations to the logical conclusion but also significantly determine the future course of Indo-Pak relations. This has been projected by army spokesperson and Gen. Kiyani himself on number of occasions in the recent past. While there indeed be justification for all this and more, considering Pakistan's past record of using such situations for obtaining and stockpiling military hardware to be used against India, there is need for care and caution.

Notwithstanding the above and many other problems and internal contradictions with which it is beset, Pakistan army can certainly be relied upon to effectively deal with the Taliban menace, once it drops its India phobia, and was provided necessary war wherewithal. However, for this to happen an allout determined and sustained thrust was the prerequisite. "Half-measures or half-hearted actions should be avoided like the plague. They haven't worked before and are not likely to succeed now". Realistically speaking and suspicions notwithstanding, the Pakistan army was an indispensable element in any successful strategy against militancy in Pakistan and the region.

The question has been raised as to why the Pak army let the Taliban ran amok and virtually halted operations against them? Pakistan's Chief of the Army Staff, General Ashfaq Parvez Kayani speaking in the 118 Corps commanders conference in Rawalpindi on 7 May 2011, observed that 'the operational pause, meant to give the reconciliatory forces a chance, must not be taken for a concession to the militants,' in an apparent reference to the lull in Swat fighting after the

Feb. 16 peace agreement. But this was only partially true. In fact, the 'pause' was under pressure from the pro-Jihadi elements within the army who argued that Taliban should be given a chance to implement the peace agreement. The other indicator was touched by him when he expressed his satisfaction at the standard and conduct of on-going training in the field formations as part of 'Year of Training' and claimed that Pakistan Army has developed full scale facilities to focus on Low Intensity Conflict (LIC) related operations.

Expressing the military's resolve to fight and eliminate the militants endangering the lives of peaceful citizens and challenging the writ of the state, Kayani urged *national concensus* to fight terrorism, extremism, "The present security situation requires that all elements of national power should work in close harmony to fight the menace of terrorism and extremism, he said. "Pakistan", Gen. Kayani pointed out, is a sovereign state and the people of Pakistan under a democratic dispensation, supported by the Army, are capable of handling the present crisis in their own national interest." He assured the nation that " Pakistan army is fully aware of the gravity of internal threat. It will employ requisite resources to ensure a decisive ascendancy over the militants."

Gen. Kiyani has got more than what he asked for. The President and the prime minister have shed their ambivalence and come out strongly and unambiguously for strongest possible action against the Taliban prompting then to hurl threats of killing of the leaders and their families. Not only that, the support for army action comes across the political spectrum. There have been public demonstration against the Taliban, some thing unprecedented in Pakistan. But what really tilted the balance was the unexpected bonanza of endorsement from the most influential *Barelvi* clerics. "We support the army operation in Swat because it is a battle for the survival and defence of Pakistan," declared Sahibzada Fazal Karim, leader of Jamiat-e-ulema-e Pakistan. On the mundane plane, the armed forces top brass also have vested interest in ridding the country of fanatic religious elements. Because there was no scope for the survival of the military's non-defence related economic empire under a Talbanised Pakistan.

As of date over fifteen thousand Pak troops are battling an estimated number of four thousand well armed Taliban in Swat, where Pakistan government has ordered a battle to 'eliminate' Islamist militants branded by Washington as the greatest terror threat to the West. "Helicopter gunships and Jet fighters shelled militant hideouts in Peochar, Shamozai and Khawaza Khela areas of Swat which started Friday night and continued until Saturday morning", a military official was reported to have said on condition of anonymity.

Be that as it may, there is no doubt that Pakistan is today engaged in fighting the mother of all battles—a war, more grave and far-reaching in its implications than any in the past. And its outcome could well determine the very future of what's left of Pakistan as a nation-state.

Pakistan is an Islamic Republic created on the basis of religion. Its Constitution says so. The mantra of nationhood is taught to every Pakistani child in the school. This has become the national epitome. On the other hand, the chain of *madarsas* which churn out armies of students each year generally bypassed the Pakistani national narrative but subjected the "talibs" (students) to a heavy over-dose of the Islamic chronicle. The products of the *madarsas* were, therefore, driven by the larger Islamic concept which defines the whole Muslim people as one nation, the *Ummah*. In the process the Pakistani nationalism was diluted and dwarfed by Pan-Islamism. The conflict between the Pakistani identity and that of an indivisible worldwide *Ummah* caricatured, to put it mildly a split nationalism in Pakistan. It is this fractured vision of nationalism which is tearing the nation and the country apart. Today Pakistan's divide encompasses not only ethnic entities, sectarian groupings but infests the country's Islamic fabric itself.

The on-going war on terrorism impacts the national identity crisis in two ways. Firstly, a large number of Pakistanis oppose the government's policy of aligning with the USA and its allies in what they perceive as the Christian war against Islam. Secondly, the ruling elite who have committed Pakistan to the international anti-terror coalition and the leadership of the security forces are consequently obliged to wage war against their own kin in the terrorist ranks. This creates a dilemma for an average Pakistani. For instance, whereas a Pakistani soldier suffers from no qualm of conscience in shooting at an Indian, or an Afghan religious denominations notwithstanding, he has a serious mental reservation in taking on his own people in Swat, Bajaur, or Waziristan. He finds the dilemma particularly unbearable when he is required to kill those claiming to be Mujahids fighting for the sake of Islam. Remember, the Pakistan army itself is groomed as an Islamic force!

On the other hand, the militants fighting in Pakistan are driven by a firm belief that the Jehad against the West and its ally, the Pakistani government is in the defence of Islam. For them, Pakistan is an *apostate* state; those who fight for the government are considered non-Muslims to be dealt with barbarously under the doctrine of *'Kafirs'*. The Pakistani soldier's ambivalence as he confronts a totally brainwashed and fully motivated pan-Islamic conviction driven Islamist breeds mental confusion and saps his will to fight. This is rated as the main cause of dismal performance of the Pak security forces in the battles raging in the North-West.

With every passing day, the mandate of the state in the tribal areas and the NWFP is diminishing. Only a couple of weeks back the militants were virtually knocking at the doors of Peshawar. The experts, mediamen, intellectuals and leaders of the fast emerging civil society alike are seriously concerned over the repeated failure to hold territory retrieved from the possession of militants after intense fighting and sacrifices. They are questioning the validity and efficacy of the planning mechanism and find the current military doctrine inept and half-cocked. The deficit on these counts, it is felt, in turn produces mental ambiguities producing ambivalence and, knee jerk, or weak response to those who challenge the Pakistan state.

The Pakistani Taliban are fast extending their reach into the heartland especially the settled area lying contiguous to FATA, Swat and Waziristan. The militancy is arching into southern Punjab which has been the main recruiting ground for the mujahedeen for Kashmir. The response in this area is reported to be overwhelming. The losses in manpower suffered in combat are not only quickly recouped by the Pakistani Taliban, but offers of volunteers exceed the losses. There is hardly any part of Pakistan which has not born the brunt of terrorists depredations including numerous Fidayeen hits. Great significance is being attached to the assault on the Pakistan's most sensitive installation and its main military arms factory in Wah Cantt. On 21st August, 2011, two suicide blasts which occurred just two minutes apart killed 70 and injured more than 80. The Pakistani Ordnance Factories at Wahh have a cluster of about 20 industrial units producing artillery, tank, and anti-aircraft ammunition for the Pakistan armed forces. It employs around 25,000 to 30,000 workers.

The war against the State and its people by militants operating under the umbrella of the Tehrik-e-Taliban Pakistan (TTP) is now undeniable. The TTP has claimed responsibility for the latest wave of bombings and is threatening more. No one, civilian, or otherwise, is safe and every murder, no matter how cruel, is justified by the TTP yardstick. The prime minister of Pakistan, Yusuf Raza Gillani himself escaped an assassination attempt on 3rd September, 2011. His motorcade was fired at near the garrison town of Rawalpindi. According to Zahid Basir, prime minister's spokesman, "At least two bullets by multiple snipers hit his armoured car." Bombing civilians inside a hospital, or outside a factory, murdering in cold blood anyone suspected of 'deviant' behaviour, slaughtering people for practising a different version of Islam, and burning girls' schools are all justifiable forms of warfare for these self-proclaimed *Jehadees*. More than two and a half lac people have already been rendered homeless. The Taliban have now asked the people to leave the troubled areas of Swat and move to safe places. The militants, according to media reports, had erected barricades on different roads and were targeting pro-government elements, especially the activists of Awami National Party that rules NWFP. In the latest outrage at least 12 people have been killed in a suicide car bomb attack at a paramilitary check-point 20 km from the north-western city of Peshawar. About 45 people were also reported wounded by the blast, most of them civilians. According to the BBC, "the attack comes after three days of continuous raids and air-strikes by US-led forces in Pakistan's tribal areas".

The civil society have had more than enough of senseless blood-shed. They demand that the government go allout to effectively curb the waves of terror sweeping across Pakistan's cities and settled areas aimed at bullying the state to back down. The backyard, where they recruit, train and equip people to inflict damage on Pakistan is Taliban's weakest spot. This fountain head of terror needs to be choked and demolished. But does the Pak army have the will and capability to do so ?

The international dimension of the Pan-Islamic militancy overshadows even the intra-Pak conflict and poses a serious though malignant threat to independence and integrity of Pakistan. The escalating militancy is souring US-Pakistan relations and bringing to fore the conflict of interest between the two partners in the war against international terror. The CIA chief, it may be recalled had sometime back, gone to the extent of identifying *Fata* as the epicentre of Al Queda terror network that targets the USA. Only the other day the Democrat Presidential candidate Barack Obama's running mate senator Joe Biden devoted part of his acceptance speech to highlight the fight against extremists in Fata. He said:

"The resurgence of fundamentalism in Afghanistan and Pakistan(is) the real central front against terrorism." He warned, "The fact is, Al Qaeda and the Taliban – the people who actually attacked us on 9/11 – have regrouped in those mountains between Afghanistan and Pakistan and are plotting new attacks." An American Government's senior analyst had earlier in August drawn attention to Al-Qaeda's success in the developing closer ties to Pakistani militants. This, according to him, had given it an extremely safe base in mountainous tribal areas. He had further disclosed that "Al-Qaeda had recruited and trained dozens 'of militants capable of blending into Western society and carry out attacks". In view of the threat perception, he had hinted that if situation so demands the US and European forces deployed in Afghanistan may not hesitate in mounting direct strikes in Fata. It is in this context that the highly unusual secret meeting on board an American aircraft carrier in the Indian Ocean on 28 August, 2009 to discuss how to combat the escalating violence along the border between Afghanistan and Pakistan has to be viewed. The day long conference was, amongst others attended by Admiral Mike Mullen, chairman of the joint chiefs of staff and Pakistan Army Chief General Ashfaq Parvez Kiyani. According to the *New York Times*, the meeting was convened by the US Chairman of the Joint Chiefs of Staff. An extreme secrecy surrounding the talks, *New York Times* said underscored, how gravely the two nations regarded the growing militant threat. Reports spoke of US concern about the security leaks from Pak ISI and emphasised the urgency of plugging the loopholes to enable restoration of mutual confidence and sharing of vital intelligence inputs.

Apparently, the Americans were not satisfied with the assurance from their Pakistani counterparts. The US-led coalition forces trespassed into Pakistan territory on 2nd Sept- and killed at least 20 people including women and children. "The Americans came in helicopters, landed, walked up to the houses, started shooting and then flew back towards Afghanistan," a villager told *Dawn*. "It is an outrage," NWFP

Governor Owais Ahmad Ghani said in a statement. "This is a direct assault on the sovereignty of Pakistan and the people expect that the armed forces of Pakistan will rise to defend the sovereignty of the country and give a befitting reply. The attack comes amid an increase in the number of missile and predator attacks on suspected Al Qaeda hideouts in Waziristan in recent days. It was the first known ground assault of its kind. He said the Pakistan Army had lodged a strong protest with the Office of the defence representative in Pakistan and said that "we reserve the right of self-defence and retaliation to protect our citizens and soldiers against aggression". Gen. Kiyani, the army chief, has demanded that the foreign forces stay away from the Pak soil. This diplomatic, rhetoric may finally end up in both countries declaring determination to jointly curb the Al-Qaeda menace. In any case the Pakistan army to whom USA has out sourced the war against terror in Fata (the last instalment received only the other day amounts to 365 million dollars) is hardly in a position to do much about it.

Caught between serious and expanding internal subversion by Tehrik-e-Taliban Pakistan and external poaching upon her sovereignty by USA and her allies, Pakistan, already neck deep in trouble, faces perhaps the worst crisis in its history. At this critical juncture, the election of Asif Zardai as the President of Pakistan places the People's Party in total control of governance in Pakistan. The leadership will need all the ingenuity it can muster to unite the party as well as the nation and mend fences with neighbours without wasting any time so that it can focus on the crucial tasks unencumbered. The outcome of its endeavours to tackle the grave crisis will not only make, or break the party but may determine the very survival of Pakistan as a nation-state.

Danger Signals from Pakistan

Zaffar Hilalai, a former Pakistan Ambassador to the United States of America was during a panel discussion on an Indian TV channel the other day provoked into speaking somewhat candidly about Pakistan's relations with Tehrik-I-Taliban Pakistan (TTP) and the Afghan Taliban (AT). "The TTP were the enemy Pakistan was fighting against", he asserted, "but we have no conflict of interests with the Afghan Taliban". According to him, at least five thousand persons crossed over daily from Pakistan to Afghanistan and vice versa with no visa, passport, or other restrictions. Pushtuns live on either side of the dividing line bound by not only tribal but also family ties. "Any animosity between the two was unthinkable", he said. Hillali, only "forgot" to add that the Afghan Taliban were the creation of Pakistan but conceded that "Intelligence agencies do not dump their assets as in a hurry". But how does this position square with Pak-US military partnership in fighting Taliban Afghanistan which in effect implied US outsourcing to Pak army the war against Taliban in the critical area at a hefty recurring cost?

Hillali disclosed no secret. In fact, the USA and Pakistan establishments as well as keen watchers of AFK-US scene were fully cognizant of the on-going game of duplicity. US and Pakistan pretended to be allies in the war against the international extremist Islamist terror blowing hot and cold as the same time as their relations waxed and waned. Obviously the aim was to make the best out of a bad marriage of convenience. Pakistan had the satisfaction of receiving the badly needed military hardware, precious allocation of funds and critical economic inputs that kept the fast sinking country afloat. America on its part gained access to military bases in Pakistan, freedom to conduct intelligence operations there and safe passage for is military hardware and critical supplies to Afghanistan. Pak army operations in Waziristan kept the Talban Pakistan fighters away from mischief in Afghanistan. Their conflict with Arab and Chechnian terrorists further help relieve pressure on US and NATO forces battling Afghan Taliban.

The uneasy relationship may have played out longer with periodical mutual recrimination providing the proverbial steam letting, but for Pak ISI acting oversmart on the crucial sticking point of the whereabouts of Osama bin Ladin. The oft repeated US allegation that Pakistan knew about Osama's whereabouts but was not sharing it with their partner and the US declaration that she was determined to take Osama out unilaterally from wherever he was found were not taken seriously by Pakistan government and its army. They forgot that eventhough the world may not be unipolar it was nevertheless subject to dictation by a superpower which openly declared that it will do everything its way, because it can. And this is exactly what US did in Abbotabad, mounted a military operation on Pakistan soil, violated Pakistan air space and sovereignty killed Osama, took his body away and buried it in high seas. When Pakistan government and military acted outraged and made unpleasant noises, President Obama reiterated his resolve to repeat such operations anywhere the wanted terrorists who posed threat to the security of the United States were to be located. This is exactly what she did through a Drone attack in Pakistan territory of South Waziristan by hitting and killing the Al-Qaeda most dreaded operational commander and Huji chief Illiyas Kashmiri along with nine others. Where do the US-Pak relations go from here? And what answers do the Pakistan government and its 'mighty' army have for an outraged and humiliated nation?

All surveys and opinion polls established that America was the most hated country in Pakistan. A more worrying dimension was brought into sharp focus by the Wikileaks, "underscoring concerns that anti-Americanism in the country's powerful military is growing amid strains with Washington." A US diplomatic cable said, "the former US ambassador to Pakistan Anne Patterson found officers at the National Defence University (NDU) were 'naive and biased' against he United States, a key ally which gives Pakistan billions of dollars of aid to help fight Islamist militants." It was further disclosed that "fears that the military could be harbouring Islamist militant sympathisers have grown since US forces found and killed

Osama bin Laden in a Pakistani garrison town, where the Al Qaeda leader had probably lived for several years."

The Wikileaks cable, published in the Pakistan newspaper, *Dawn* quoted Patterson as saying, "The elite of this crop of colonels and brigadiers are receiving biased NDU training with no chance to hear alternative views of the US "Given the bias of the instructors we also believe it would be beneficial to initiate an exchange programme for instructors". Apparently, Pattersons' proposal of exchange programmes though worth trying could hardly be the solution. May be even for the limited purpose it was too little too late. The grievous affliction and its advanced stage demanded nothing short of a major surgery.

What should be a real cause for anxiety not only for the USA but also for neighbouring India is that the commanders at the critical level of colonels and brigadiers of Pakistan army, were infected or being infected with the deadly virus of militant Islam of the Al Qaeda variety. The Pak Army High Command appeared to be unable, or unwilling to effectively intervene to stem the rot. As it is, the Pak Army has a history of failed extremists coups, which is perhaps the best kept secret of the army next only to the long list of VVIP assassinations. Incidentally, the fact that four former Naval officer convicted for helping the militants in attacks on defence facilities, were languishing in a prison in Rawalpindi was revealed by the Pak Geo TV after they were questioned about the attack on PNS Mehran.

Pakistan was today precariously poised on the brink of a precipice. The very future of the nation-state was hanging in the balance. The civil society, the intelligentsia, the media and other liberal enlightened segments were acutely apprehensive about the future of the nation and the country. They read the danger signals loud and clear but were at the moment unable to craft a unified and comprehensive response. "Whether it was a US induced intelligence failure, or outright incompetence of our own sleuths is immaterial. What matters is that the Osama episode has put us in a hole and we first need to claw our way

foundation conclave. American investigators had collected a mass of evidence of deep linkage between these anti-India terror groups. Many experts on terrorism have forcefully and unambiguously asserted that the Lashkar was inspired by the success of Al-Qaeda in rallying supporters for a global *jihad*. Lashkar fighters were sighted in Afghanistan and Iraq fighting and killing Americans.

Al-Qaeda was waging war against what it called the Christian-Zionist-Hindu combine "out to demolish Islam". Osama bin Laden declared war on India through the 13 April, 2006 audio taps released by Al-Jazeera, wherein he spoke of "a crusaders-Zionist-Hindu war against the Muslims". "It is the duty of the *Ummah*" he said, "with all its categories, men, women, and youth to give away themselves, money, their experience and all types of material support to establish Jihad." The 26/11 dastardly assault on India's financial hub Mumbai bore unmistakeable signatures of the dreaded Al-Qaeda. All the three enemies of Islam-Christians, Jews and Hindus listed in the tapes were hit on 26/11 in Mumbai in a single clean composite comprehensive and focussed operation.

Lashkar-e-Toyba, "army of the pure," was promoted by Pakistan, "the country of the pure" in early eighties as a proxy force/strategic asset and unleashed in Jammu & Kashmir to "undo Muslim-dominated Kashmir's accession with Hindu dominated India". "This is a group that years ago evolved from having a local and parochial agenda and bought into Al-Qaeda's vision," said Bruce Hoffman, a professor at Georgetown University who had followed the fortunes of the Lashkar for several year.

The Lashkar had for long been on the US State Department's list of foreign terrorist organisations, which described it as one of the largest and most dangerous terrorist outfits in South Asia with close links to the Taliban and Al-Qaeda. The department also maintained lists of a dozen odd group used by the LeT to cover up its true identity. Many US counter-terrorism and military officials felt it was necessary to reassess the capability and spread of the Lashkar after the assault on Mumbai. They agreed that it posed a much greater threat than previously recognised even though Headly connection was still under deep wrap at that point of time. But the drift continued.

The Al-Qaeda organisational structure was strategically fashioned as a global network linked to already existing, or contrived indigenous extremist groups. It operated through such affiliates especially in countries where favourable environment for the presence and operations by its own cadres did not exist. While the international anti-terrorist coalition led by the United States nibbled at the fringes and remained enmeshed in complex and sterile games in AF-pak region, the Queda caravan kept steadily moving forward achieving enormous extension of its network across the globe. There was hardly any part of the world where its tentacles had not reached, be it Asia, Europe, or Africa. Its sizeable presence in Netherlands, Belgium, France, Spain and Germany and ever increasing capability to do mischief was giving sleepless nights to the law enforcement agencies and respective governments. The growth and spread in Africa under the banner of Al-Qaeda Maghreb has been phenomenal. Al-Qaeda had spawned countless cells of potential terrorists exploiting the power and anonymity of internet technology. In the UK alone the authorities were reported to have detected over 200 separate plots of indiscriminate criminal activity.

Al-Qaeda operating under the cover name of the World Islamic Front had access not only to the well organised, fully equippend, intensely committed and highly motivated affiliates like Lashkar-e-Toyiba but also enjoyed the support of the powerful Pak army. Pakistan undoubtedly remained the epicentre of Pan Islamic terror machine and its Waziristan belt the training as well as battle inoculation hub for recruits from all over the world. They were frantically striving to extend control and clout world wide, enhance military prowess, upgrade weaponry and communication capability. Quest for dirty nuclear bombs was being pursued vigorously. Reports suggest that Al-Qaeda already had access to chemical warfare stockpile.

The huge terror threat posed by burgeoning Al-Qaeda can be ignored by the civilised world at great peril. But possessed by passion for short term interests in Af-pak region, the USA has got enmeshed in a quagmire. Lashkar-e-Toyiba, an integral part of Al-Qaeda led World Islamic Front was the strategic asset of Pak army, which also had closest ideological and strategic links with the Afghan Taliban. United States of America engaged in fierce war against Al-Qaeda-Taliban combine generously funded and equipped Pakistan army to which she had practically outsourced the fighting against Taliban on this side of Khyber pass. Despite being fully aware of this particular Axis of evil, the USA played along Pakistan thus becoming instrumental in strengthening the very Al-Qaeda, the coalition was fighting in costly war in Afghanistan. The other dimension of the draconian drama was exposed by the Wiki Leaks.

There is a lot to be disturbed by in the battlefield reports from Afghanistan released by "Wiki Leaks. The close-up details of war are always unsettling, even more so with this war, which was so badly neglected and bungled by President George W. Bush." "But the most alarming of the reports were the ones" he says that described the cynical collusion between Pakistan's military intelligence service and the Taliban. Despite the billions of dollars the United States has sent in aid to Pakistan since Sept. 11, they offer powerful new evidence that crucial elements of Islamabad's power structure have been actively helping to direct and support the forces attacking the American-led military coalition. How long this charade will take to play out was anybody's guess. In the meantime, the Al-Qaeda was quietly but quickly spreading its influence and firming up hold on the African continent. They were reportedly consistently gaining ground. If Al-Qaeda were to succeed in striking deep enough roots, bring most of the barbaric African tribes under its wings and USA did not abandon the current suicidal Af-pak policy in time, the war in Afghanistan would look like a picnic in comparison to the horrors that conflict in Africa would unfold.

Pak-US Relations: Will the History Repeat itself once again?

The escalating militancy in Fata, Waziristan and adjoining areas is souring US-Pakistan relations and bringing to fore the conflict of interest between the two partners in the war against international terror. In fact, the relations between the two countries were currently going through a very bad patch. Pakistan was even perceived by the US establishment and the Congress as "not doing enough to deliver on the war against Taliban Afghan as well as indigenous". The strong feelings in USA were understandable as the Pak military operations against Taliban were being financed by that country. The last instalment of $ 365 million was recently transferred to Islamabad. Actual and budgeted amounts of US aid for Pakistan during period 2001-08 totalled to $ 5.174 billions.

The CIA chief, it may be recalled had sometime back gone to the extent of identifying Fata as the epicentre of Al-Qaeda terror network that targeted the USA. Only the other day the Democrat senator Joe Biden devoted part of his speech to highlight the fight against extremists in Fata. He said: "The resurgence of fundamentalism in Afghanistan and Pakistan(is) the real central front against terrorism. "The fact is Al-Qaeda and the Taliban—the people who actually attacked us on 9/11— have regrouped in those mountains between Afghanistan and Pakistan and are plotting new attacks." He warned an American Government's senior analyst had earlier in August drawn attention to Al-Qaeda's success in the developing closer ties to Pakistani militants. This, according to him, had given it an extremely safe base in mountainous tribal areas. He further disclosed that " Al-Qaeda had recruited and trained dozens of militants capable of blending into Western society and carry out attacks". In view of the threat perception, he had hinted that if situation so demands the US and European forces deployed in Afghanistan may not hesitate in mounting direct strikes in Fata. The international dimension of the Pan Islamic militancy over-shadowing even the intra-Pak conflict was pregnant with a serious though malignant threat to the independence and integrity of Pakistan. It is in this context that the highly unusual secret meeting on board an American aircraft carrier in the Indian Ocean on 28 August 2008 to discuss how to combat the escalating violence along the border between Afghanistan and Pakistan had to be viewed. The day long conference was, amongst others attended by Admiral Mike Mullen, chairman of the joint chiefs of staff and Pakistan Army Chief General Ashfaq Parvez Kiyani. According to the *New York Times*, the meeting was convened by the US Chairman of the Joint Chiefs of Staff. An extreme secrecy surrounding the talks, underscored, how gravely the two nations regarded the growing militant threat. Reports spoke of US concern about the security leaks from Pak ISI and emphasised the urgency of plugging the loopholes to enable restoration of mutual confidence and sharing of vital intelligence inputs. This was followed by yet another visit to Pakistan by Admiral Mullen, the CIA top brass and the states department. There were also doubts (sometimes more than doubts) about the sincerity and commitment of sizeable and powerful segments of military hierarchy especially the ISI, believed to still be working in cohorts with Taliban on both sides of the Durand. The mistrust persists despite these high level confabulations.

Apparently, the Americans were not satisfied with the assurance from their Pakistani counterparts. The US-led coalition forces trespassed into Pakistan territory on 2nd Sept. and killed at least 20 people including women and children. "The Americans came in helicopters, landed, walked up to the houses, started shooting and then flew back towards Afghanistan," a villager told Pakistan daily *Dawn*. "It is an outrage," NWFP Governor Owais Ahmad Ghani said in a statement. "This is a direct assault on the sovereignty of Pakistan and the people expect that the armed forces of Pakistan will rise to defend the sovereignty of the country and give a befitting reply". The attack came amid an increase in the number of missile and predator attacks on suspected Al-Qaeda hideouts in Waziristan in recent days. It was the first known ground assault of its kind.

A Pak security official told *Dawn* that the Americans no longer shared information with them before launching missile, or predator attacks in the tribal region. "They are not sharing any information with us. These are all totally unilateral actions." Inter-Services Public Relations chief Maj. Gen. Athar Abbas said. The army spokesman condemned the "completely unprovoked act of killing" and regretted the loss of precious lives. He said the Pakistan Army had lodged a strong protest with the office of the defence representative in Pakistan and said that "we reserve the right of self-defence and retaliation to protect our citizens and soldiers against aggression". There was, in fact, an incident of firing on a coalition forces gunship by Pakistan army which was explained away as "non-lethal warning shots" aimed at conveying that the aircraft had dangerously strayed close to Pakistan territory. Despite the bravado, the Pakistan army to whom USA, the sole superpower had outsourced the war against terror in Fata etc was obviously handicapped in formulating and executing a serious and strong response The missile hits and attacks by NATO drones based in Afghanistan had become routine. Apparently, the issue remained unresolved.

Two factors decisively impact the validity and efficacy of US-Pak joint venture against Pan Islamic fundamentalist terror and will determine the future of the coalition. Firstly, Whose war is Pakistan fighting in Fata and elsewhere? Is it the American war hoisted upon Pakistan, or is it the war for survival of Pakistan itself as a nation state?

The militants operating under the umbrella of the Tehrik-e-Taliban Pakistan (TTP) made no secret of their war against "the apostate" Pakistan State. The TTP had claimed responsibility for the waves of bombings and was threatening more. No one, civilian or otherwise, was safe and every murder, no matter how cruel, was justified by the TTP yardstick.

Shafqat Mahmood addressed this dilemma in his write up titled, "Whose war is it anyway?" published in *Dawn*. "Those who blame the Americans for our current troubles are right because without the Afghan war in the eighties, the large-scale mobilisation and arming of militants may not have happened. They are wrong when they say that people currently challenging the Pakistan state are only doing it because of the American invasion of Afghanistan in 2001 and Pakistan's subsequent partnership with it in the war against terror", he pointed out. "This factor has certainly contributed to the anger of the Pashtuns in Afghanistan and their kin in the tribal areas of Pakistan but the conflict in Swat, Bajaur, Hangu, Darra Adam Khel, Khyber agency etc. is not because of the Americans and neither is the Marriott bombing." He asserted and went on to say, "It is a handiwork of people who are determined to impose their version of an Islamic state. Much before the American invasion Sufi Mohammad in Bajaur wanted to impose Islam. People like Fazalullah in Swat are his close disciples and actually related to him. They are not blowing up girl's schools because they hate the Americans. The reports reveal that the Taliban have forced closure of 125 girl's schools in the area under their control and blasted the school buildings imparting education to the girl students was decreed un Islamic. Hundreds of girl students have joined hostels in the settled areas to pursue their studies. They, however, remain apprehensive about the safety of their parents back home. Such is the intensity of terror. Their compatriots are not asking people in Peshawar and other parts of the Frontier to stop wearing trousers, or shaving or listening to music, or watching television because they have America on their mind. They are doing it because they have a certain vision of a state and they want to impose it by force. "The truth was that the Pakistan leadership was hardly left with any option. The space to determine whether the country will fight terrorism to ensure the survival of the Nation State, or capitulate before Pan-Islamism was shrinking very fast.

With her economy in shambles, the polity fractured, social structure torn asunder by poisonous sectarianism and rampant confusion at the top political echelons, Pakistan just cannot afford to let the downwards slide in her relations with USA to continue beyond a point. "There is a pattern in US-Pakistan relations. For last 60 years they have gone through cycles of massive aid followed by threats of sanction and then application of sanctions." Pakistan has been an ally of the United States during the cold war, in the war of resistance against the Soviet occupation of Afghanistan and currently in the global war against terror. Each period of close US-Pakistan ties began with great hopes and ended up in tremendous disappointment for both sides", wrote Hussain Haqqani, Director, Boston University's Centre for International Relations. And the history has a bad habit of repeating itself.

Bounty on Hafiz Sayeed. What is the American Game Plan?

The US Hafiz Sayeed bounty bomb has turned to be a dud, at least for India and for the present. The $10 million bounty announced by the Obama administration was "aimed primarily at shutting down Sayeed's terrorist operations even as Washington attempts to bring him to justice for the Mumbai carnage". A bare reading of the Rewards for Justice notification issued by the US Justice Department, which announced "upto $10 million" bounty for "information leading to the arrest or conviction of Hafiz Sayeed" makes it amply clear. All lingering doubts were set at rest by official clarification that "an informant could be eligible for a Rewards for Justice reward payment if his or her information were to lead to Sayeed's conviction in any US or foreign court of law for his terrorist acts". Thus this notification, trashed the evidence provided by the Government of India to Pakistan (with which United States are fully conversant), the disclosures made by their own citizen Headly in the US court and the mountain of evidence procured by American intelligence agencies. In effect, the US position regarding the value of evidence provided by India against Hafiz Sayeed in 26/11 Mumbai terror attack is perilously close to that of Pakistan.

His elimination is implicitly discounted. The contrast with the "wanted" notice posted against Ayman-al-Zawahiri and others calling for their outright elimination is too stark to be missed. So as of today the United States has no intention to bodily harm much less eliminate Pak ISI's protégé and one of world's most dangerous terrorists, Hafiz Sayeed, the ideologue and supremo of Lashkar-e-Toiba whose cadres were engaged in terror-strikes across the globe. The "I love US" brigade will, therefore, be well advised to do some homework before getting into "balley-balley" mode.

The US double speak becomes apparent from the State Department's categorical statement that Hafiz Sayeed "participated in the planning of the four-day long terrorist attack." A media note circulated by the State Department affirmed that "Sayeed and his organisation continue to spread ideology advocating terrorism, as well as virulent rhetoric condemning the United States, India, Israel and other perceived enemies. The question is Why is the US administration taking contradictory positions? And what exactly is the game plan?

Does the US expect that the notification of the bounty will compel Hafiz Sayeed to shelve any future mischief even if it does not result in his conviction for the Mumbai carnage ? Too naive to merit any serious consideration. As it is, Sayeed seldom goes beyond his "safe houses" in Lahore and Islamabad/ Rawalpindi, which ensures he is beyond the reach of American Drones. He certainly knows what is good for his health. The Hafiz refused to take the bait offered on national television by a Pakistani law-maker to preach his anti-American message in Fata and face elimination by a hellfire missile instead, the Hafiz burrowed himself in the garrison city of Rawalpindi where his official security cover was enhanced by the Pakistan authorities. From the safe haven of the city that houses the Pakistani Army's headquarters, he challenged the US to come and get him.

Why was he, Lashkar supremo and master terrorist, spared a death warrant? No official explanation is coming forth. The reasons however were not far to seek, Washington does not want to aggravate the situation with the Pakistani security establishment, which was known to be the father, mother and wet nurse combined of the Lashkar-e-Taiba/Jamaat-ul-dawa and diligently protected its supremo. It is also interesting to note that amidst all this high voltage drama Deputy Secretary of State Tom Nides landed in Pakistan to hold talks with the government to restore, normalcy in the over-wrought ties between the two sides. This incidentally, was the first high level initiative by the US government to engage Pakistan's badly fractured and military-driven government since the Salala check-post shoot out which cost Pak army lives of her 24 soldiers. In retaliation Pakistan closed down the supply routes critical for the NATO forces battling Taliban in Afghanistan.

Pakistan public opinion was broadly wearing around to the views expressed by Hafiz Sayeed in an *Associated Press* news agency interview quoted by BBC News are of 14 April, 2012 that "the US only announced the reward because of his demonstrations against reopening supply lines through Pakistan to NATO troops in Afghanistan". Writing in the *Wall Street Journal* (India Edition of 3 April 2012 Tom Wright qouted Haji-Sayeed saying "The US is frustrated because we are staging strong protests against resumption of NATO supplies and Drone strikes. It was talking to Qatar based broad caster Al Jazeera. But this is only part of the story. The other dimension is that by notifying the bounty on Hafiz Sayeed but stopping short of issuing a death warrant, the US government is also serving the notice to Pakistan to keep the Hafiz and his goons at bay and open the supply routes to Afghan front. Failure to comply will invite notification of death warrants for Hafiz and Makki and may be couple of more Lashkar commanders and their execution. These steps may also be reinforced by financial, armament and economic sqeeze, consequences where of the tottering Pakistan government already at the verge of bankruptcy cannot even dare to visualise.

We in India must remember that moves like Hafiz bounty, reference to 26/11, of course, emphasise on the killing of 6 American citizens and intermittent laudatory references to India and critical comments against Pakistan were essentially tentative in nature. These in no way reflect decisive shift in US-Pak policy. Till the stage of final US-Pak disconnect is reached and America decides to dump Pakistan as the front line strategic ally India has to intimately watch out for her own national vested interests in the region and indeed the countries on its periphery. Our military strategy, diplomatic manoeuvres and economic/commercial and security initiatives should be designed and executed with our own resource for our own objectives and for the good of our own country. If any international initiative happened to support, or reinforce our actions, it may be welcomed as a bonus.

12

Assassination of Benazir Bhutto

Return of Benazir Bhutto

After eight long years of self exile, two times prime minister of Pakistan and chairperson of the Pakistan People's Party, Benazir Bhutto arrived in Karachi on 18th of October, 2007 to a tumultuous welcome. This was expected.

She faced an imminent threat to her life on arrival. No less a person than President Musharraf had implored her to postpone her return. Benazir had also been warned by a friendly foreign country' of the conspiracy to eliminate her on her return to Pakistan. She had "written to President Musharraf on 16th of October and named three conspirators, two of them men in power." This was disclosed by Benazir herself. Pak authorities have since acknowledged the truth of the assertion. So all this was known. The measures adopted by the Pakistan government, if any to at least 'isolate them' and ensure that they were not able to meddle with the security arrangements made at Karachi on the fateful day remain shrouded in secrecy and therefore subject only to conjectures. The authorities have evaded answers to the persistent and pertinent media queries in this behalf.

If the regime attempted to impede the PPP's mobilisation to greet Benazir in any major way, not much is known about it. In fact, the PPP leadership was consulted by the authorities while devising the security arrangements. The establishments' suggestions to tone down the size and character of the reception and proceed from the Airport to Mazar-i-Quai-i-Azam by helicopter were, rejected for obvious reasons. As the *Dawn* commented editorially, "Those who criticise her for not delaying her return, or even for coming back in such grand fashion miss the point that the leader of a national political party who returns home after an exile of eight years, can hardly be expected to be whisked quietly away to her home by a handful of supporters."

That the threat to her person was grave and imminent was conceded all around. The authorities were, therefore required to take speedy and effective measures to gain actionable intelligence about the specifics of the terrorist's plans through standard procedures so that the evil designs could be thwarted, or at least the damage minimised. It would also have been fruitful to co-ordinate with the "friendly country" which had tipped Bhutto in the first instance. Having been forewarned they were in an advantageous position the terrorists having lost the crucial element of surprise. As the events unfolded, it was clear that the government had either not performed adequately, or it had miserably failed in the sphere of intelligence collection. Even the text book measures in this kind of situation necessitated extensive, intense and intimate surveillance of all suspected and known terrorist of the anti-Bhutto variety and mount massive vigilance and activate standard physical and technological counter measures to deny the terrorists any opportunity to execute their nefarious plans and be stopped in their tracks. None of this happened. The most glaring lapse was the failure to mount an aerial surveillance which could have enabled identification of suicide bombers in time.

The attack did take place, but for the steadfastness, strong sense of loyalty and vigilance of the Security Guards of the Pakistan People's Party (recruited from amongst the ex-policemen and ex-servicemen loyal to Bhutto) the terrorists may well have succeeded in their nefarious designs. It turned out Bhutto's bullet-proof vehicle was protected by two security cordons. The inner cordon was manned by Benazir's personnel and private security men. It is learnt that the PPP leaders had taken a firm and uncompromising position that only their men will man the inner cordon rubbishing the argument of the authorities that the government security personnel were better trained etc. The outer cordon comprised of officers and men of Sindh Police and plain clothed personnel of Pakistan Intelligence Bureau. By now it is known that the suicide bombers were not spotted by the policemen posted along the route and peppered in the crowd. In fact, they were able to walk through the Sindh Police-IB cordon with ease which speaks volumes. They were, however, sighted by PPP Security Guards. Unable to penetrate their cordon they blew themselves up.

For obvious reasons the protection of the person of Benazir Bhutto had to be accorded the topmost priority. An impregnable protective umbrella had to cover, apart from other vantage points of enroute and the points of reception and termination of the cavalcade. Physical and technological surveillance over the suspects atomization of 'moles' within terrorist outfits and coordination between various intelligence agencies to speedily gain actionable intelligence were some of the routine steps required to be taken with a view to prevent and abort the attack on Benazir. What measures were taken in this regard is not known. However, the suicide bombers came perilously close to attaining their objective which testifies to the failure of the establishment. Bhutto had a providential escape, thanks to the exemplary sense of loyalty shown by her party security guards.

Her critics accuse her of being plain stubborn and reckless in "throwing all caution to winds and invite trouble not only for herself but for thousands upon thousands of her supporters to almost certain terrorist strike? She brushed aside the suggestion that she take a helicopter ride from Karachi airport to the Mazar of Quaid-e-Azam. But she did it for important and politically sound reasons. "If nothing else," writes Aasim Sajjad Akhtar in his piece titled 'Who rules the roost' in *Jang*, "the relatively raucous reception given to the twice former prime minister by tens of thousands of people on the streets of Karachi points to the fact that the Pakistan People's Party (PPP) and its chairperson remain a major political force in the country. It should also be a signal to other political entities—which wax lyrical about street power—whose actions speak louder than words"

Benazir has been asserting that all her endeavours including negotiations with President Musharraf were aimed at working out a road map for "transition from dictatorship to democracy". The democratic rights of the people of Pakistan were at the core of her concerns. Her detractors argued that there were no takers for her 'apologia' for securing withdrawal of corruption cases pending against her and that the political environment had drastically altered to her disadvantage during the eight years she was out of her country. Ironically, her political opponents notably PML(Q) had begun to believe in their own propaganda knowing fully well that even in the 2004 elections universally recognised as massively rigged, PPP had secured 25.8 per cent votes, the highest tally.

After she decided to return to Pakistan and the establishment decided to let her come, Benazir had only two options, (1) To go by the official advice which would result in total destruction of her hard earned image as a fighter and bury her fathom deep as an epoch making leader. (2) To risk a terrorist attack on her person in the belief that people's power will come to her rescue. Somewhere in the back of her mind there must also have been the expectation that President Musharraf after having mended fences with her would rein in the mischief mongers.

Predictably, Benazir opted for the second course of action. The sea of humanity that greeted her and thronged the eight kilometre long road from Karachi airport to Mazar-e Quaid-e-Azam bore testimony to the validity of her decision.

Through her bold decision, she has not only struck a mighty blow for democracy but also brought into play the dormant peoples' power that blasted the wishful and self-serving political projection of her opponents. With one single stroke she has brought the people of Pakistan on to the centre stage casting aside the fear and so called invincibility of the military dictatorship and its political minions. Of course, the revolutionary change has come at a heavy price, 140 dead and over 500 injured.

Her triumphant return negated the calculations of the ruling party that having been 'marginalised' Benazir could be 'managed' to play a role of the junior partner. Panic stricken, they lost all control and sense of proportion and set upon a confrontation course even using foul language against her person. Apart from the fear that an adverse Pakistan Supreme Court judgement will invalidate Musharraf's election as President, the apprehension that she will sweep the Choudhary brothers and their PML(Q) into the dustbin of history was the most important factor that led to the imposition of what has been described as Emergency Plus in Pakistan triggering the on-going turmoil in that unfortunate country.

Musharraf-Benazir Deal

Did US Facilitate Bhutto's Assassination?

At this point of time it is difficult to identify with any measure of certainty the real US objectives in brokering Benazir Bhutto's return to Pakistan ending her eight years self-exile. Remember, it took a painful and violently fluctuating process of negotiations by US officials including assistant secretary of state Richard Boucher around year and a half flying forth and back between Dubai, London and Islamabad to "clinch the matter".

What exactly was the Bush administration's game plan? They were dealing with Benazir Bhutto, the daughter of the East, twice prime minister of Pakistan undoubtedly the only

Pakistani leader whose clout extended to the entire federation. Even in last elections to the national assembly universally, recognised as atrociously and totally rigged her Pakistan People's Party obtained maximum votes even though she herself was unable to lead the party in electioneering. Did the Bush administration intend to promote the cause of democracy in Pakistan and decisively project her as the authentic voice of the people in a country hostage to the whims and fancies of their protégé, dictator Muharraf, whose popularity grading had touched the rock bottom? Or was Benazir to be used as an instrument to perpetuate the dictatorship of their Man Friday, General Musharraf and in the bargain defame, demoralise, devalue and discred this mass leader by projecting Benazir as a feeble and unprincipled politician willing to do the biding of both the patron state, the US of A and her Pak minion to escape the wrath of law in corruption cases pending against her? Such image devastation would push her to the margins of Pakistani political arena. Moreover, by jumping on Musharraf's sinking ship she would be inviting the popular wrath directed against Musharraf for his self-invited confrontation with the Pakistan Supreme Court in March last in which the Dictator was truly and squarely humbled. Such diversion would naturally afford some relief to a besieged Mushaaraf, who would have by then doffed his uniform.

For obvious reasons, perceptions on this count varied. According to Gwyner Dyer eminent Independent Journalist (Pakistan, Politicians, judges and General May, 14, 2008) "The plan was that Musharraf, by now a deeply unpopular figure in Pakistan, would allow a controlled restoration of democracy in which another close American ally, Benazir Bhuttoo, would return from exile and become prime minister. For historical reasons her Pakistan People's Party stood a good chance of winning a free election. Afterwards, she would work together with Musharraf, now a duly elected civilian president, who would step back from the limelight but still exercise ultimate control over the military".

The New York Times (19 October, 2007 editorially commented as fallows.

"After belatedly recognizing that the general's misrule was dangerously strengthening, not weakening, extremist forces in Pakistan, Washington helped engineer the deal that permitted. Ms. Bhutto's return. Now, it must help her and Pakistan truly move toward democracy".

"The U.S. came to understand that Bhutto was not a threat to stability, but was instead the only possible way that we could guarantee stability and keep the presidency of Musharraf intact," said Mark Siegel, who lobied for Bhutto in Washington and witnessed much of the behind-the-scenes diplomacy" (*New York Times*-updated April, 16, 2010).

"I am returning to Pakistan on Oct. 18 wrote Benazir Bhutto in her piece 'When I return to Pakistan' to bring change to my country". "Pakistan's future viability, stability and security lie in empowering its people and building political institution. My goal is to prove that the fundamental battle for the hearts and minds of a generation can be accomplished only under democracy." She asserted and went on to say that "The central issue facing Pakistan is moderation vs. extremism. The resolution of this issue will affect the world, particularly South and Central Asia and all Muslim nations. Extremism can flourish only in an environment where basic governmental social responsibility for the welfare of the people is neglected. Political dictatorship and social hopelessness create the desperation that fuels religious extremism'...(*Washington Post* September 20, 2007). It should be apparent that US establishment saw in Benazir as a dependable and strongally in the high stake was against international terror as well as the ongoing conflict in Afghanistan in conjunction with the Pakistan Army. Pak Army leadership was perceived as not averse to working with her and dumping Musharraf who had become a liability. Bhutto, on her part had always made a distinction between army as an institution and individual Generals driven by lust for political power. The involvement of

General Parvez Kiyani, the current chief of Pakistan Army in the negotiations with Bhutto tended to give credence to this line of reasoning. Incidentally, Kiyani as a junior officer had served as deputy military secretary to Bhutto and thus enjoyed a kind of proximity to her.

Musharraf was known to be reluctant to grant amnesty not to speak of sharing power with her. Benazir's presence in Pakistan was particularly dangerous for him as his public rating plummeted and the Supreme Court of Pakistan, the Bar, the media and the intelligentsia became more and more demanding and defiant. In the scenario when he faced the very real prospect of being dislodged from the Aiwan-i-Sadar by a "hostile" Supreme Court, democracy crazy Benazir Bhutto was the last person he could countenance.

Then there was the rag tag collection of Musharraf's minions bundled under the label of Pakistan Muslim League (Q). Ironically, they had begun to believe in their own propaganda that the political environment had drastically altered to Benazirs 'disadvantage' during her eight years exile conveniently forgetting that even in the 2004 elections which they had so successfully and massively rigged, PPP had secured the highest tally of votes. President of PML(Q) Choudhry, Shuj'ahat Husain and his cousin Pervez Ellah, the then Chief Minister of Punjab were known to have a cosy relationship with the Jihadi elements. "The Choudhries of Punjab must be restrained", wrote Aisim Sajjad in *Jang,* Karachi, "from announcing large sums of money that will go into looking after the children and the extended family of a cleric who engaged in terrorism against the people in his immediate vicinity and the state at large." "The religious right", he went on, "may be the Choudhries" original constituency, given their people-unfriendly politics, but offering the worst rightist elements financial support in an election year and under the circumstances is mind-boggling. Terrorism under whatever pretext must be abhorred, condemned and dismissed as an agent of change."

For the Choudhries and their hangers on, Benazir's return and the public response she was getting in their own "stronghold" Punjab, spelled doom. As disclosed by the then railway minister Abdul Rashid, they had vociferously opposed the Reconciliation ordinance that made Banazir's return to Pakistan possible, but deferred to the wish of the Master albeit reluctantly. The boss was reported to have reassured them that he "will handle every thing". Their agenda was simple and unambiguous. They did not want Benazir around at the time of elections.

The US officials claimed that they kept her fully and regularly informed of the grave security threat. Musharraf sang the same tune. The USA surprisingly resisted her attempts to arrange private security from the West on the specious plea that the presence of foreigners will attract "greater" attention when she was already known to be the topmost target. Zardari and Benazir refused to engage local private security agencies as suggested by US officials for sound reasons. Their apprehension that these agencies were more likely than not infiltrated by ISI agents was genuine and real. The Chairman of the Senate Foreign Relations Committee, senator Joseph Biiden, told a press conference in Iowa that he had personally interceded with Musharraf to ask for specific security procedures to protect Bhutto but his requests were ignored.

In the absence of any direct evidence of his complicity in the assassination it may be fair to assume that the denial of the requisite security cover to Benazir by Musharraf was tactical, the calculation being that shaken after the attempted assassination of 18th October and finding her exposed and vulnerable, she might take the exit route leaving the political arena open to him and his cronies for manipulation of the electoral outcome. This was easily the most immature and flawed reading of Bhutto's personality and mental make up

Benazir, on her part, was clear and categorical about her political agenda. She publically asserting that all her endeavours including negotiations with President Musharraf were aimed at working out a road map for "transition from dictatorship to democracy". The democratic rights of the people of Pakistan were at the core of her concerns. She contemptuously brushed aside the insinuations that she was simply bargaining for withdrawal of corruption cases pending against her and tellingly pointed out that not an iota of evidence had been held against her in Pakistan courts for more than eight long years. Her conduct of the campaign for democracy, the 18th October, 2007 nearly successful assassination attempt, denial of the basic security cover and harassment by the government including restrictions on her movements, house arrests etc. notwithstanding was aggressive and focussed. She was a fighter and an uncompromising crusader for democracy. The people loved her for that high voltage and even higher decibel campaigning and came forward in droves in a powerful passionate response. She gave voice not only to the suppressed people of Pakistan but galvanised the democracy loving people all over the world. Alarmed at her stunningly successful campaign and the special cord she struck in the hearts of men, women and children of Pakistan, the vested interests struck on 27th of December as she emerged from a mammoth rally in Rawalpindi snuffing her life flame and plunging Pakistani nation in unprecedented collective mourning. The US press "credited" secretary of state Condoleezza Rice for persuading Benazir Bhutto in October last to return to Pakistan to implement the arrangement brokered by the US with Musharraf after the Reconciliation Ordanance had been issued dropping all cases against her. In doing so, they lamented, Rice sent her to her death.

Benazir Bhutto is no more but the flame of hope and courage to strive for democratic rights she had so painstakingly and courageously kindled in the hearts of the suppressed people of Pakistan burns bright and strong. Even her worst enemies line up to pay tributes to the "Mohtarma". In death, she acquired the stature of an icon reserved only to the creator of Pakistan, Quad-e-Azam Mohd. Ali Jinnah.

The manner in which the US administration handled the whole affair culminating in the terrible tragedy of Benazir Bhutto's assassination raises many questions of which answers may never be found. It is, however, clear that neither democracy in Pakistan nor peace in the region was anywhere near the top of the US agenda. Raw and short sighted national self-interest was the sole motivation.

Obviously, the US establishment was fully aware of the ground realities and temper of times and the critical juncture in its history. Bhutto also had to make a choice. She preferred to take a chance with physical elimination. In essence, whether by dereliction or design the US, significantly contributed to the assassination of Benazir Bhutto. In the process it pushed a major chunk of Pakistani nation represented by PPP fence sitting into the widely the patties. Yet they launched Banazir Bhutto their most precious asset in an suicidal enterprise that could end up either in her demise as an effective political entity, or her physical elimination. Having returned to Pakistan with her own agenda in the momentous prevailing and fast swelling anti-American space. Anti-Americanism is the only sentiment in Pakistan today. "Just about every Pakistani with whom I spoke blamed her death not on Al-Qaeda but on their own government and the United States" reported Philadelphia Inquirer columnist Trudy Robins from Pakistan. He had hit the bull's eye.

Who is Responsible for Assassination of Benazir and ongoing Coverup?

Benazir Bhutto, the first lady prime minister of an Islamic country a controversial political personality at best of times—became a national icon on achieving martyrdom in the Garrison town of Rawalpindi on 27th December last. Her assassination plunged the nation into collective mourning cutting across the regions, religions, parties and sect divides. As the news of her assassination spread like wild fire a massive wave of grief swept through the length and breadth of the country. Men, women and children rushed out of houses weeping and wailing. Pakistanis, emotional people as they are, let their grief gush out in full measure unabashed and uncontrolled. Benazir emerged as the symbol of national unity in a country at the verge of destabilisation and dismemberment. She achieved in death what remained a distant dream in her life time. Today friends and foes vie with each other to pay her homage and acclaim her death as a national calamity.

The thorough professionalism and superb military precision were the hallmarks of the assassination of Benazir Bhutto. The manner and efficiency with which the physical evidence at the scene of crime was systematic and comprehensive destroyed left no doubt that the endeavour was integral to the main operation. Significantly, the task was accomplished sequentially with thoroughness which does not come naturally to the official agency (The Fire Brigade) detailed for the job done. The level of arrogance and immunity from norms was in full play as the task which would itself be a crime under the law was committed in full public glare. The Video footage showed it all. It particularly focussed on a pistol lying on the ground almost touching the ammunition Boot of, perhaps the sole uniformed man visible at the scene at that point of time. The disposal of the weapon and the identity of the man in uniform is still shrouded in mystery. The recovery of the weapon in whatever condition and identification of the official could help push for a break through.

Lt. Gen. Hamid Gul, former Director General of the ISI said, he was shocked at the spectacle of people watching the hosing down of vital evidentiary clues from the crime scene which is routinely sealed all over the world. "It is a crime scene and they are washing away all the evidence ! We need to be asking why the hell was this thing done"? he demanded. An equally pertinent question should be who authorised the destruction of evidence and why? In fact, the identification of the source of authority for this part of the operation could, perhaps provide an opening that the Scotland Yard team is groping for.

The tentacles of the OPS 'Cover up' reached out to the hospital where Benazir Bhutto was taken after the attack and officially declared dead. Video footage available showed a senior doctor of the hospital disclosing that when Bhutto was brought to the hospital her pulse, heartbeat and breathing had stopped. There was "big injury" on one of her temples and the skull was fractured. In conclusion he said, "when something hard strikes the temple with great speed such symptoms are present. The heart stops causing death." Sherry Rehman, Press Secretary of the PPP, who was with Benazir at the time of assault also stated that Benazir had sustained a "big bleeding injury" on the temple. "There was lot of blood in the car", she said. The video footage confirmed her statement. She was also one of the ladies who performed the ritualistic last bath. "The big wound had not been cleaned and the blood was still oozing therefrom" she stated. 'The big injury', which no one cared to clean could arguably be the exit point of the bullet that hit Benazir if the entry wound is seen in the X-rays again depending on their genuineness. The Ministry of Interior, however had other ideas. Its spokesperson Brig. (retired) Iqbal Cheema first claimed that Bhutto was hit by a shrapnel released by the explosion. Within hours he shifted the stand. "At the time of explosion Bhutto was waving to the crowds through the sun roof of the bullet Proof Car. She ducked down and in the process banged her head against a protruding Lever fitted in the vehicle causing fracture to her skull and her death". Very convenient. It implied that Bhutto herself was to blame for the tragedy. In fact, the Pakistan establishment has been hyper-active in spinning out distortions, half-truths fabrications and down-right lies apparently as part of a cover up. The assassination was, however, handled with gross immaturity. It lacked the professional skill and finish and left many faces in red as one fabrication after another was exposed by incontrovertible documentary and witness evidences.

The first sign of the web of lies coming apart became visible when the Interior Minister distanced himself from the position taken by his official spokesperson following the release of amateur footage showing a clean-cut man in black vest brandishing what clearly resembles a gun. Behind is seen another man whose head is covered by a scarf. He was believed to be the suicide bomber. The Punjab government subsequently issued front page advertisement in newspapers offering a reward of one crore of rupees to anyone giving information leading to their apprehension.

And now a semblance of truth appears to be tumbling down from the horses' own mouth. In an interview with the US television network CBS, a cornered and somewhat sheepish President Musharraf admitted for the first time that the martyred Benazir Bhutto, may have been hit by assassin's bullet. Asked if Ms. Bhutto might have been shot, he answered, "Yes, absolutely, yes. Possibly". Whatever terminology a cagey Musharraf opted for, the admission was unmistakeable. This rubbished albeit reluctantly, the yarns spun out by the Pakistan Interior Ministry spokesperson, Brig. (R) Chemma. As it is, there were no takers for either his "shrapnel hit theory", or the infamous assertion that the lever on the sun roof had caused the fatal injury when she ducked following the explosion. The video footage available had conclusively established that Benazir's head was not exposed in the sun roof at the time of explosion allegedly set off by a suicide bomber. The manufacturers of the bullet-proof car had categorically stated that there was no metallic lever fitted in the car that could have caused the injury. The forensic experts also discounted the possibility of death resulting from a strike with the lever. Musharraf's latest pronouncement has also proved right all those who alleged that doctors in the hospital where Benazir was taken after the attack were pressurised to fudge the reports to fit the Interior Ministry theories. Both Chemma and Musharraf, however have not deviated from the primary but totally untenable position that Benazir Bhutto was herself to blame for the tragedy by literally sticking her neck out of the sun roof. *Prima facie,* this was a crude attempt to exonerate the Pakistan government of the responsibility for her assassination. In essence they peddle a theme that is as preposterous as it is heartless. A senior PPP leader, senator Babar Aiwan responded, "I feel that there is a skeleton in the cupboard of the government and that's why they have been changing their stance. From day one we have been saying that she was shot. It was a conspiracy, a plan executed, we have absolutely no doubts about it." Asked by CNN's Wolf Blitzer whether Bhutto had not been reckless, Mark Siegel shot back, "Don't blame the victim for the crime. Musharraf is responsible." It was to Mark that Benazir had e-mailed a message shortly after the 18 October last assassination attempt at Karachi when she returned to Pakistan after more than 8 years. In her e-mail she said that she would "hold Musharraf responsible" if she were killed in Pakistan. "I have been made to feel insecure by his minions." She wrote, "There is no way that what is happening in terms of stopping me from taking private cars, or using tinted windows, or giving jammers or four police mobiles to cover all sides could happen without him." Senator Joseph Biden, chairman of the foreign relations committee and a candidate for the democratic presidential nomination held a press conference in Iowa in which he revealed that he had personally interceded with Musharraf to ask for specific security procedures to protect Bhutto but the request was ignored. It is significant that jammers when provided were non-functional. These were neither replaced nor repaired despite requests and remained non-functional till the fateful day.

It is obvious that Bhutto was not provided reliable and standard security (whatever may be Musharraf's concept of adequate security). Denying even her request for private security speaks volumes. It may also be instructive to compare the levels of security in place for Musharraf and late Benazir Bhutto, the most threatened politician in Pakistan at that point of time. According to threat perception both were on top of the hit list. But then whose hit list are we talking about?

In any case, whose responsibility it was to ensure that the protected person was insulated at the point of embarkation? When a person openly brandishing a pistol and another presumably a suicide bomber smoothly and without any constraint gain access within hitting distance of the VIP, the government and only the government becomes accountable for the lapse.

The video footage also gives lie to Musharraf's claim that adequate security was provided. Senator Babar Aiwan, who was with Benazir on the fateful day is on record that only one Deputy SP and three constables were available on the spot of the tragedy.

Deputy Superintendent of Police Ishaq Hussain Shah, who was on security duty with Benazir Bhutto on th fateful day (apparently the officer senator Aiwan was referring to) is currently recuperating from serious injuries at the Combined Military Hospital, Rawalpindi. He told *Dawn* that the Walk Through Metal Detecting Gates installed at the venue of the PPP Rawalpindi rally on 27th December last had stopped functioning "due to power cut shortly before she was assassinated". Remember, the electricity shut down had also occurred in Karachi on 18th October last just before the first assassination attempt on Bhutto. Shaw confirmed having spotted "a man wearing sun-glasses standing about three meters from Benazir Bhutto's car and was firing at her with a pistol." "As soon as I jumped to overpower him, a mighty explosion occurred", he stated.

A jubilant Benazir was accompanied by senator Babar Aiwan, Sherry Rehman and another person as she walked down with a broad smile pasted on her face. The exit route was absolutely secure. So where was the crowd of thousands of her supporters following her as alleged by Musharraf? This was yet another figment of Musharraf's imagination. The truth is revealed by Dy. SP Shaw. The officer who was on the left side of Bhutto's vehicle said, "he saw some people appear from nowhere and stop the car while she was leaving Liaqat Bagh".

And very significantly added, "I don't know who they were, or from where they came. They were carrying flags of the Pakistan People's Party and shouting pro-PPP slogans. They just appeared on the road". Who permitted, or facilitated access to the restricted area that was supposed to be cordoned off? In these circumstances, one is apt to wonder, Could the sudden appearance of "some people carrying PPP flags" be the refined version of the failed attempt at Karachi on 18th October?

Before she landed at the Karachi airport, Benazir had written to President Musharraf and identified certain persons in authority in the government from whom she apprehended threat to her life. The then chief minister of Punjab, Ch. Parvez Ellahi and the Director of Pakistan were prominent amongst them. Instead of ensuring that they had no role and exercised no authority in respect of anything even remotely concerning Benazir Bhutto, they were conferred greater confidence and authority by the President. President of PML(Q), Choudhry Shujahat Hussain and his cousin Pervez Ellah, the then chief minister of Punjab were known to have a cosy relationship with the pro-Jihadi elements in the defence establishment, especially the ISI as well as with Brig. Shah. The brigadier had a very colourful background. He was reputed to have been the handler of both Osama bin Laden and Mullah Umar during his stint in the ISI. No wonder the assailants had free passage through the Sind Police-IB outer cordon in Karachi on October 18th last. But for the vigilance and quick response by PPP security guards the attempt may well have succeeded on that day itself.

"It is time Gen. Musharraf realised that many of those awarded ministries and key roles under his tailor-made political dispensation are in effect the religious right's Trojan horses in his administration. The government should be required to make an about-turn, this time not for furthering the objectives of the US-led global war on terror but to save its own people and the state from falling to medievalism in the garb of religion," Wrote Aisim Sajjad in Daily Jang Karachi referring to Choudhry cousines, Shujahat Hussain and Parvez Elahi.

Abdul Rashid, the then Railway Minister of Pakistan and a close confidant of President Musharraf told a Pak TV Channel that "most of cabinet ministers were opposed to the Reconciliation package which included withdrawal of corruption cases against Bhutto and paved the way for her return to Pakistan. "It was with great difficulty that the President was able to persuade them to fall in line; the most vociferous in opposing the "deal" with Benazir were the Choudhry cousins." Musharraf himself has conceded that Benazir returned to Pakistan against his advice. It is by now clear that Musharraf and his coterie did not want her to return to Pakistan. When she did return they tried to trivialise the occasion by frightening her to confine her activity to address the party workers at the airport, then take a helicopter ride to the Jinnah Mausoleum, pay her obedience and quietly go to her home in Larkan. The real crunch came when she insisted on going for a tour of the Punjab. And indeed reached Rawalpindi and fixed a rally in the Liaqat Bagh. This caused panic in the PML(Q) leadership of Punjab. If the PPP were activated and workers enthused through her rallies their very political survival would be in jeopardy. They could not risk their stolen fiefdom of Punjab being stormed. Hence her house arrest in Rawalpindi etc. As she remained defiant, refused to relent and was in fact making waves throughout the country someone had to do something about it before it was too late. Rest is history.

The circumstances surrounding the assassination of Benazir Bhutto and the developments since her landing in Karachi on 18th October last stink of a sinister conspiracy to eliminate her by men in high positions in the governmental and political hierarchy. As it is, the history of Pakistan abounds in cover ups of assassination cases of top leaders. The impressive "roll of honour" includes the first prime minister of Pakistan Liaqat Ali Khan, Military Dictator Zia-ul Haq, and Army Chief Asif Nawaz. Unmistakeable signs of a massive cover up operation are discernable. On the positive side, national and international public opinion and leaders and workers of the

Pakistan People's Party are closely monitoring the progress of investigation and antics of the authorities. The newly emerging civil society and a keen, fearless and watchful media have already exposed the lies and half truths the authorities were busy pedalling as part of the cover up conspiracy. Concern in this regards openly expressed by the UN, the West especially, the USA, the European Community and the UK has already forced Musharraf to involve the Scotland Yard in the investigation of the assassination case. Still there is need for utmost constant vigilance and brutally frank timely response if the unvarnished and full truth behind her assassination is to be unmasked in entirety.

13

Who is Behind the Air Crash that Killed PAF Chief?

The mood in the fundamentalist camp in Pakistan is upbeat. This is attributed to the unexpected and unprecedented success of the six Islamic fundamentalist parties combine – the Mutthahida Majlis-e-Amal (MMA) – in the last elections to the National and Provincial Assemblies. The Majlish has further consolidated gains in the by-elections. The MMA is today the largest Opposition group in the Pakistan National Assembly. The MMA is also in power in the sensitive North-West Frontier Province (NWFP) and a coalition partner in Balochistan bordering Afghanistan, the scene of a massive hunt by the US troops and their local collaborators for the Al-Qaeda and the Taliban. This unproductive and frustrating hunt for Osama bin Laden, Mullah Omar, their close aides, numerous wives, sons and sons-in-law has only dwarfed the mighty United States in the eyes of the common man. The aura of invincibility has vanished. The mutual mistrust and strains in the relations between the Pakistan Army and the US military chasing the Al-Qaeda in Afghanistan, the Pak-Afghanistan border and on hot-pursuit into Pak territory has exploded into the open.

The current anti-US upsurge on the issue of Iraq, evidenced by two 'million marches', has lent further impetus to the wave of pan-Islamic fundamentalism. So has the ISI strategy to 'hunt with the hounds and run with the hares'. The Pakistan Government, led by the lackadaisical Mir Zafarullah Khan Jamali, possesses neither the will nor the capability to stem the fast-gathering tide of the aggressive and defiant Pan-Islamists. The prime minister dare not even strain at the leash firmly held by President Musharraf, who is keeping a poker face. No wonder the ongoing power struggle for dominance over the military machine has considerably sharpened in recent days. The *jehadi* elements in the Pak Defence Services have intensified their activities and extended their field of operations. They feel more confident than ever before.

The nuclearisation of Pakistan, modernisation and up-gradation of the Pakistan Air Force have radically altered the equations within the Pakistan defence setup. The Pak Air Force, a poor cousin till the other day, rates as an equal with the Army, its diminutive size notwithstanding. The Pakistan Air Chief, who operationally controls the nuclear arsenal delivery system, has, in the changed circumstances, acquired enhanced clout and prestige. His alignment with either of the groups contesting for the control of the Pakistan war machine would make all the difference when the chips are down. This makes the Pak Air Chief the most sought after as well as extremely vulnerable personality. It is in this politico-military context that the air crash near Kohat that killed Air Chief Marshal Mushaf Ali Mir, his wife and aides has to be viewed.

On February 20, the Pakistan Air Force Fokker-27—carrying Pakistan Air Force Chief, Air Marshal Mushaf Ali Mir, his wife Begum Balquees, and fifteen others including Air Marshals Safim Nawaz and Razzaq, Air Commodores Raja Rizwan and Javed—crashed near village Taulanj, 27 kms from Kohat in the North-West Frontier Province (NWFP). There were no survivors. The Pak Air Chief was on his way to Kohat for the annual inspection.

According to Pakistan Air Force spokesman Air Commodore Sarfraz Ahmaed Khan, the plane, a part of the VVIP squadron of the PAF, was certified as "flight worthy" and technically cleared before it took off from the Chaklala military airbase at 8 am. The last contact between the Kohat control tower and the crew was at 8.27 am when the permission to 'descend' was sought. Significantly the Pak Air Force spokesman maintained that "the PAF would neither rule in or rule out any cause for the accident". He repeatedly appealed to the media not to speculate and wait for the findings of the high-level inquiry ordered by the PAF. Air Marshal Asghar Khan (R), the first Pakistani Chief of the Air Force, appearing on the PTV the other day, emphatically asserted that the Fokker plane was a very sound and reliable machine thereby excluding the possibility of any technical snag. Obviously, the plane carrying the Air Chief could not but be flown by the very best team of fliers on the rolls of the Pakistan Air Force. So, if the flying machine was sound, the plane was certified 'flight-worthy' and 'technically cleared' just before take off from the Chak lala air base, what caused the crash?

Media reports speak of eye-witnesses having heard an 'abnormal sound' from the Pakistan Air Force (PAF) Fokker air plane 'in the misty atmosphere' before the plane 'suddenly fell with an explosion'. What caused this 'abnormal sound'? Perhaps the identification of the 'sound' and tracing the source of its emission may provide a clue to the real cause of the crash. It needs to be emphasised that from all accounts, the ill-fated plane at the time of crash was having a normal trouble-free flight. It was, in fact, in the process of descending under acceptable weather conditions. The Kohat Military Air Base is a much used facility. The low hills surrounding the air base neither pose any hurdle to landing, nor hold any surprise for the fliers. Air Marshal Mushaf Ali Mir (55) enjoyed the reputation of a thorough professional in the traditional mould. He was said to be completely free from the *jehadi* taint. He was also ambitious. A 'no-nonsense' commander, Air Marshal Mir was certainly not in the good books of the *jehadi* mafia who were currently engaged in a major bid for 'dominance' in the Pakistan Defence Services. Incidentally, Air Marshal Mir is the first Chief of the Pakistan Air Force (PAP) to become the victim of an air crash. It is significant to note that while the Pakistan Air Force spokesman was pleading with the media not to speculate about the cause of the crash and await the findings of the high-level probe which, in his own words, would "neither rule in, nor rule out any cause of the crash", the PTV came out with a categorical announcement that "the plane crashed due to technical reasons'. This was no ordinary plane crash to be given the routine treatment. The victims of the crash included the Chief of Air Force, his Begum and two other Air Marshals. Here two questions arise. Who authorised this 'announcement'? This obviously had to be done at the highest level. And why were the high and mighty in the Pak establishment in such a desperate hurry to pre-empt the findings of 'high level inquiry committee'? The sharp contradiction between the positions taken by the Pakistan Air Force (PAF) and the state-controlled Pakistan Television creates ample grounds for suspicion. This crack in the otherwise well-crafted 'solid case' tends to swing the needle of suspicion towards *jehadis* inside as well as outside the Pak power structure.

The Kohat area where the plane carrying Air Marshal Mir and party crashed is literally crawling with fundamentalist zealots, Taliban supporters and Al Qaeda agents. That the provincial Muttahida Majilis-e-Amal, Government patronised these extremist elements is an open secret. They are known to have access to all kinds of sophisticated weaponry including 'land-to-air' missiles. Were the *jehadi* elements responsible for the tragedy that claimed the life of Air Marshal Mushaf Ali Mir, his wife and others? Only an impartial, competent and deep probe could provide an answer.

The so-called high-level probes in Pakistan have a history of concealing rather than revealing the truth. Question marks till date hang on the truth behind the air crash in which, among others, the then Pakistan dictator General Zia-ul-Haq perished. The veil from the suspected poisoning of General Karamat, the then Army chief, is yet to be lifted. Much may, therefore, not be expected from the exertions of the high-level Pakistan Air Force inquiry even though the United States experts are collaborating with their Pak Air Force counterparts.

The United States of America has vital stakes in the outcome of the ongoing tussle for control of the Pakistan war machine between the 'professionals' and the *jehadis.* The ever-widening gulf within Pakistan Military High Command has the potential of exploding into open confrontation. Such an eventuality would completely and irreversibly upset all US calculations. It was, therefore, only natural that the Americans endeavour to dig up the truth of the Kohat air crash. The reports of an independent, *albeit* discreet, probe by the US experts into the crash should thus surprise no one. For obvious reasons the United States cannot countenance a *jehadi* takeover of the Pakistan war apparatus. Such a development would, in fact, spell disaster for the US national interests in South and Central Asia and severely hamper her international anti-terrorist thrust. The United States, therefore, would do all that it takes to abort the *jehadi* grand designs in Pakistan. Moreover, if it were to be established that the air crash that killed Air Chief Marshal Ali Mir was the handiwork of *jehadis* of whatever hue, a whole lot of significant and far-reaching US political and military initiatives would be unleashed. The existing equations in the region will be upset. Even regimes may be toppled. President Bush in his recent utterances has left no one in doubt that the United States could go to any extent to protect her national interests.

14

Polls that Ousted the Dictator

How Fair were PAK Elections?

The Pakistan political scene has been undergoing a somewhat imperceptible transformation for the last three years, or so. The unprecedented freedom of the press and people to people contacts with India were perhaps the potent factors that helped explode the pent up yearning for democracy. Lalu Prashad Yadav's reaching out to the common man during his visit to Pakistan did the trick. If a 'rustic' like Lalu Yadav, it was argued, could rise to become the chief minister of Bihar and then the railway minister, in democratic India, why should political power in Pakistan remain the hand maiden of the privileged elite and the Generals in Pakistan? But, Musharraf surrounded by sycophants, and serviced by army of minions felt secure in his world of "make believe" behind the high walls of the Aiwan-e-Sadar. The monarch of all that he surveyed failed to perceive or gauge the dramatic change in the mindset of the restless and increasingly frustrated citizenry. The evidence of his being totally out of tune with ground realities convincingly came forth when he humiliated the Chief Justice of the Supreme Court, Iftikhar Choudhry and placed him under suspension in March last. The Chief Justice had to be reinstated following massive sustained and widespread civil society protests and international condemnation. This retreat marked the first serious setback for the then military dictator. But fears of an impending adverse judgement culminating in his ouster from the presidency prompted a panicked Musharraf to promulgate the Provisional Constitutional Order and impose Emergency in the country in the capacity of Chief of the Army Staff. As the chief justice and overwhelming majority of his companion judges of the Supreme Court expectedly refused to take oath under the CPO, they were not only replaced by those willing to do the bidding, but also placed under house-arrest. The murder of independent judiciary became a critical issue in the elections. A captive judiciary could be relied upon to reject any judicial challenge to his election. Thus a tight web was woven to close all avenues of redress for those who may chose to contest the irregularities and downright rigging before, during, or after the polls. Significantly, the election commission announced that there will be no 'progressive' declaration of election results. Musharraf's threats that protests against the election results will not be tolerated and sternly dealt with, left little to imagination regarding the purpose and import of these manoeuvres.

An in-depth survey of Pakistani public opinion was conducted by world public opinion.org in collaboration with US Institute of Peace from Sept. 12-18. This was just before President Pervez Musharraf declared a six-week state of emergency and before the assassination of former Prime Minister Benazir Bhutto. The survey revealed majority support for a moderate and democratic Islamic state. Only an insignificant, minority showed sympathy for Islamist militant groups. The martyrdom of Benazir Bhutto firmly placed democracy at the centre of popular concerns as never before. Obviously, there could be no democracy without an independent judiciary and dictatorship and democracy were clearly incompatible.

But Musharraf was not convinced. He repeatedly referred to the West's 'obsession' with democracy during his pre-election European tour. It was not the first time that he uttered such sentiments in public. Political analysts feel that they served as a disturbing reminder that even after almost a year of traumatic events in the country, he had made no attempt to recognise an age-old cure for the many evils inherent in the current political system. Had the situation not been so grave in Pakistan, it might have been easy to brush off the president's comments as yet another myopic observation. "Unfortunately, we are already at the brink, and the rejection of a true democratic order–yes, indeed, like the West's, with emphasis on fundamental rights and civil liberties for all, and not one that is tailored to meet the president's vision–can only aggravate", said the experts.

In an article in the Asian Tribune, Asif Haroon Raja, an eminent security analyst said there was need to replace "sham democracy with true democracy suitable to the geniouss of people of Pakistan. The only answer to this crisis is genuine constitutional democracy. Even the army leadership appears to understand this reality", "...Despite Pakistan having been burdened with the politico-ideological baggage of the international anti-soviet *jihad* of the eighties, its experimental wisdom has brought the overwhelming majority of Pakistanis to the conclusion that the only way forward is the rule of law; that while faith and identity were intrinsic to ones being the only way for the state to conduct the affairs of society and politics is legal and constitutional way", he concluded.

Fearing peoples wrath and a sympathy avalanche in favour of the People's Party of the assassinated leader, Musharraf postponed the elections to 18 February, 2008. A full fledged operation "rigging" was mounted. Three institutions critical to the conduct of free, fair and impartial elections the election commission, the government and the judiciary were meticulously and comprehensively subverted. The handpicked Election Commission had demonstrated its subservience to Musharraf in 'managing' his election to presidency and during filling of nomination papers to the national and provincal assemblies. The supposedly impartial 'care taker' government was headed by Samru, a sitting senator elected with the support of Pakistan Muslim League (Q), known as the King's party. The country's judiciary was in shambles, the chief justice, the judges and leaders of the bar locked up and its independence torn to shreds. What Musharraf did to Pakistan judiciary was not only unprecedented but a disgrace for any regime that laid claim to democratic credentials and rule of law.

If the elections turned out to be a referendum on the future of General (R) Musharraf, he alone was to blame. Having 'fixed the election commission and the Judiciary' and placed his hand picked men at the helm in a so called Care Taker government, he was satisfied that the King's party would sweep the polls. In this he grossly miscalculated and miserably failed to assess the mood of the Pakistani people. He wantonly and aggressively threw his full weight behind the party of 'his' government and went about beating the drum of its unprecedented performance in the field of development. He openly violated the universally recognised code of conduct that mandated that after the electoral process was notified no new schemes be announced, no projects activated, or fresh projects inaugurated. He believed all this will do the trick. Probably, his options were shrinking. His entire future depended on the outcome of elections. To his utter horror, however, the people of Pakistan categorically rejected him and his PML(Q) placing a big question mark on his future.

The "fairer than expected", or shall we say "fairer than feared" polls on the 18 February testified to the resurgence of the people's power and project civil society as powerful determinant of the fate of the Pakistan, a country that, had for too long been led by the nose by military dictators. The transition was not easy. It exacted a very heavy price in tremendous suffering and sacrifices by known and unknown crusaders in the cause of democracy, human rights and revival of secular traditions. The brave, the determined and the dedicated men and women alive and still fighting and those who became martyrs in these illustrious causes deserve to be saluted by all freedom loving people of the world.

Musharraf's plans went haywire because the people were not intimidated by the large scale deployment of forces and the threat of their use. This balloon had been pricked by Army Chief General Kayani, who ordered the army to maintain distance from politicians. His men were just not available to do the dirty work. It was clear that the army as a institution was more interested in preserving its popular image rather than inviting people's wrath to serve the interest of an individual.

The credit for the 'fair election' is deserved by the determined voters, aware and committed political activists and the Pakistan army, who remained neutral, its massive deployment and known position proved a crucial deterrent against the planned massive rigging. Even the pre-poll rigging proved to be of no avail.

The polls were certainly not completely fair. Selective rigging was resorted to in constituencies where the margin of victory was considered "manageable". The desperation and frustration on the part of those detailed for "managing" soon degenerated into panic as the tide turned. Many instances of fake voting were caught on the camera and corroborated by documentation. The video footage telecast by a private Pak television channel showed stuffing of votes by individuals who looked like IB men. In one instance a man was seen making a female voter exercise her franchise at pistol point. The channel confronted the election commission with the evidence. The commission representative understandably evaded the issue by claiming that he has not viewed the telecast.

Post-Poll Dispensation in Pakistan

Will Democratic Concerns and Army Interests be Harmonised?

A trinity of three A's – Allah, America and Army, it has been said determines the fate of Pakistan. Its affairs are run according to its dictates. Everything was going fine till March 2007, when the then Chief of Army Staff and the President of

Pakistan decided to court serious trouble by summoning the chief Justice of the Supreme Court of Pakistan to the Aiwan-e-Sadar. Ch. Iftitkhar, the chief justice, was apparently not amused by the humiliation heaped upon him. One thing led to another. An enraged dictator, not used to even disagreement not to speak of defiance, did the unthinkable. He created history of sorts by placing the Chief Justice of the country under suspension on charges of 'corruption', which at the best were tenuous and flimsy.

Even before Musharraf had time to sit back and begin to gloat over his imperial prerogative and a sample of the exercise of the immense powers that he wielded, all hell broke loose. A defiant chief backed by the Bench and an outraged fraternity of' bar across the country picked up the gauntlet. Pakistan witnessed the spectacle of lawyers, media persons, academics, human rights activists and members of the fast emerging civil society streaming into the streets in strong and sustained protests unknown in its history. The action of the dictator also attracted universal condemnation including from one of the crucial As - the United States of America. His patron in the White House pointedly called upon him to back out.

The dictator finally had to beat a retreat and re-instate the Chief Justice. This signaled the. emergence on the socio-political scene of Pakistan of yet another and mightier A - the *awam,* the people of the Pakistan. They have since left no one in doubt about their determination to script their own destiny. A desperate dictator resorted to the imposition of Emergency, gagging the media and letting loose repression of the worst kind. This proved a bigger disaster resulting in the martyrdom of Benazir Bhutto. In her death she struck the biggest blow for democracy. The entire nation demanded democracy and nothing less. This was how Benazir would have liked to avenge her assassination. The elections though strategically postponed had to be held. The result of the polls confirmed a vote for democracy and independence of judiciary. It also mandated that Musharraf goes.

The question today was not whether Musharraf will go but how and when? Will he remove himself or be removed from the Pakistan political scene ?

Post-Pak polls, America was speaking in different voices. The White House attempted to burden Musharraf with the undeserved credit for holding "fair elections" and was exerting all its influence to put together an arrangement in which Musharraf continued to remain the President of the country and played a key role in the war against terror. The academia, the media, the think tanks and other organs of opinion makers in USA including an influential segment of the establishment have, however, seen the writing on the wall. Even otherwise, they were not impressed with Musharraf's record of fight against Al Qaeda and Taliban. They recognised that he had to go but would prefer to wait till a viable alternative was found and readied to be put in place. Remember, this was the election year in USA and the exit of much discredited President Bush was a settled fact. Contradictory signals from various power centers should, therefore, surprise no one. Having said this, it would be only realistic to recognise the critical role and clout of USA in determining the future political set up in Pakistan. While the country was important to the United States for security reasons, Pakistan's economy and military were precariously propped and decisively dependent on the USA. The withdrawal of the props would spell disaster for the Pak economy.

General Ashfaq Parvez Kiyani's pre-poll directions to the army officers to refrain from meeting politicians and focus on their professional duties set the tone of Pakistan army's future role. Newspapers also reported that army officers deployed in civil departments were being recalled to their units. More importantly, in his address to the corps commanders the current Chief of Army Staff pointed out that "it is the harmonisation of the socio-political administrative and military strategies that will usher in an environment of peace and stability in the long run. Ultimately, the will of the people and dispensation they support will prevail. This marked a major and radical shift from the policies so far pursued. The concept of 'harmonising' broadly defines the basis, the contents and contours of the future "power sharing arrangements" that may be worked out between the political leadership and the Army GHQ in the days to come. It will, obviously, be naive for anyone to interpret distancing from politicians as directed by Gen. Kayani to mean surrender of the pivotal role in the affairs of Pakistan by the army as one of the key stakeholders. It should be hoped that the new political dispensation as well as Army leadership will address this crucial issue realistically, patiently and with political sagacity. An arrangement, it should be hoped, will be arrived at that addressed the security concerns of people of Pakistan and also made its transition to full fledged democracy smooth and certain.

15

Winds of Change Blowing Across Pakistan

The war against the Taliban by the Pakistan army was inherently handicapped for want of the popular support. The common man's perception was that the Pakistani soldiers were being pitted against their own kin to serve the interests of the hated Americans. This was considered the most formidable and almost insurmountable obstacle. The impossible had, however, happened. The Taliban themselves did it.

After they successfully brow beat the Pakistan government and national assembly into notifying the Nizam-e-Adil regulations for Swat, the Taliban overlords, Mufti Mohammad, Fazlullah, Baitullah Mehsood and their ilk became reckless and threw all caution to winds. They violated all and every clause in the agreement and declared democracy and other attributes of the Pakistan Nation state as unIslamic. Becoming ever more emboldened, they demanded the hand-over of all the seven districts of Malakand division and Kohistan district. Unmindful of the consequences, they started implementation of their intolerant, divisive and brutal agenda and recklessly launched intrusion into adjoining areas raising hackles not only in Pakistan but also in the rest of the world. There were talks of Taliban takeover of Islamabad and imminent threat to country's nuclear assets. The blowing up of *ziarats* and bombing of mosques while the faithful offered prayers provided the proverbial last straw on the camel's back. The people of Pakistan woke up to the grave threat to their lives and liberty. As veteran Pakistani journalist Ahmed Rashid put it, Pakistan was facing a major existential crisis: "I no longer say that there's a creeping Talibanisation in Pakistan, it's a galloping Talibanisation". (Pakistan is facing galloping Talibanisation *Dawn*. Com. 5.4.2009 - Featured Articles).

The differences regarding their genesis and motivation, notwithstanding considerable unanimity had emerged in Pakistan that the Taliban posed a grave threat to the very existence of the Pakistan as a nation state and the unity of its Islamic society. The emerging consensus was that they can't be allowed to impose their despicable and divisive version of religion by force, as they attempted to in Swat.

Prime Minister Gilani's announcement of the decision to call out the armed forces "to eliminate the militants and terrorists in order to restore the honour and dignity of the homeland, and to protect the people" could not have come at a more appropriate time. The change in government policy towards Taliban may have been prompted by the consensus arrived at the tripartite Af-Pak strategy meetings presided over by President Obama. Such a categorical reassurance was, in any case, absolutely necessary because of the public perception that "while the political government was indecisive and dithering, the Pakistan army operations were half-hearted and botched." Motivation and the circumstances that led to the shift in policy will perhaps be debated for a long time to come but the threshold had been crossed. In fact, the decision to confront Taliban head-on could easily become a historical landmark in Pakistan's quest for the state that judiciously combined elements of modernity, sterling liberal Islamic ethos and responsive and responsible democratic governance.

Gen. Parvez Kiyani, the chief of the army staff, who bears the grave responsibility of implementing the Diktat of the Pakistan Federal government did well to bluntly state that 'the present security situation required that all elements of national power should work in close harmony to fight the menace of terrorism and extremism". His intention obviously was to make it clear that the government and other concerned could not wash their hands off after issuing directives because the army alone could not win the war against terrorism. It would need the active support and sustained backing of all other elements– the government, the civil society the political class and the liberal clergy.

The realisation that the very existence of Pakistan was under threat provoked deep introspection in the thinking community. In an article titled 'Unheeded lessons of democracy' published in *Dawn* on 19 May, 2009, Niilofur Farrukh reminded the nation that "dictators may have deprived us of our vote from time to time, but we as a nation have contributed to a system built on nepotism, expediency and convenience. Pakistanis clamour for democracy during dictatorships yet make a mockery of adult franchise when less than 30 per cent of the voting population casts its vote. Our tolerance for bribes, kickbacks, illegal commissions etc. has reached an alarming level. So it comes as no surprise that Pakistan ranks among this planet's five most corrupt countries. Institutions, both in the public and private sectors, that could have served as the building blocks of democracy, have been turned into personal fiefdoms with little regard for the mandate they have been given to serve." Disgusted with the prevailing situation, she quoted humorist Imran Aslam's portrayal of the core values in a play that "we are a country where ideas is a departmental store, Liberty is the name of a market, and Freedom and Trust are personal hygiene products" and saids, "May be it's time to ask if Pakistan was ever a democracy, or have we rapidly slipped from being a colony to an oligarchy constituted by a powerful, dishonest and self-serving elite that connives at monopolising politics, land, the military and industry. The conspiracy to keep the majority disenfranchised is clear to anyone who has lived through, or studied the country's short history." The collective conscience of Pakistan was being pricked.

The Sunni Tehrik activists were perhaps the first to organise public protests all over Sindh in mid April, rejecting the enforcement of Nizam-e-Adil regulation by Taliban in the NWFP through brutal force and use of gun. They reminded the religious zealots that Islam spread through love and forgiveness, and not terror. "Islam is a religion of tolerance and piety and renounces oppression of all kinds", they declared.

Its Sindh, convener Maulana Noor Ahmed and scores of Tehrik activists came out wearing shrouds to condemn the sacrilege of shrines and killing of Pir Sharifullah Mujjadidi in Swat and Ajmal Darbari in Mirpur khas. Maulana Ahmed was aghast as to how blood-thirsty law-breakers could be expected to guarantee peace and justice. "How come people unaware of the essence of *shariat* can enforce it through gun and powder and which religion allows killing followers of sects, other than theirs," he demanded and said, "it's disgusting to see the Taliban indulging into bombing and rocket attacking places, sacred to followers of other sects".

Pakistan's moderate clerics, who remained mute witnesses to the escalating fundamentalists barbarities for years were now mobilising support for the government as it battled the Taliban. "The military must eliminate the Taliban once and for all," Mufti Sarfraz Naeemi, a senior cleric of the moderate *Barelvi* school of Sunni Muslims, told Reuters. "Otherwise they will capture the entire country which would be a big catastrophe." Mufti Naeemi claimed that the *Barelvis* had so far kept silent and endured the Taliban oppression because 'they wanted to avoid confrontation between Muslims. "But they could not stand by and let the Taliban impose their rule", he said. "We don't want civil war...But God forbid, if the government fails to stop them, then we will confront them ourselves", the Mufti declared. It was a highly significant development because most of Pakistan's 160 million people from whom the armed forces personnel were drawn belonged to the *Barelvi* school.

The army operation *Rah-e-Rast* was making headway in Swat. The Mingora headquarter of Fazlullah had fallen and was in ruins. The Taliban commander, possibly wounded, was running scared. The Taliban strategy of bombing civilian targets in NWFP and beyond to spread terror as retaliation for the losses suffered in Swat had backfired. The people were not terrorised. Instead the anger and abhorrence against the senseless blood letting was mounting with every terror strike. On the home turf in the western parts, elders of the Allai Tehsil decided to wage a war against militants if they tried to infiltrate into their territory. "We are the guardians of our motherland and if the militants tried to enter our area, we will teach them a lesson. The militants will never be allowed to disturb the peaceful environment of our area," vowed members of the grand *Jirga,* which was held in the backdrop of possible infiltration into Allai of the militants fleeing from the neighbouring districts. They issued a decree, asking the people not to allow the militants on their soil and foil their bid for infiltration into the area.The elders warned that if anyone provided shelter to the militants, he would not only be expelled from the area forever, but also his house would be set on fire. They made it clear that every matter would be settled in accordance with the Pakhtun traditions to ensure complete peace and harmony among all the tribes. In many places local Lashkars formed to battle Taliban were chasing and killing them. The hound was being hounded.

"The Pakistan political class, including many of the religious parties which earlier nursed a soft corner for the Taliban appeared to have sensed the dangers posed by them. Politicians are realising there is no future for the country if the militants continue to expand their influence," said retired general and analyst Talat Masood. The moderate clergy was also feeling threatened because their role will be over under a Talbanised dispensation. This convergence of national and self-interests was providing the vital trigger to the fast changing Pakistan scenario. The views of the emerging and strident middle class, the intelligentsia and the dominant section of the Pakistan media about the reality of Islam in the sub-continent was aptly summed up by Ajaz Ameer, "Talibanism is a menace and a threat to our way of life. There's little room for any dispute on this point," he wrote in *Dawn* and asserted, "In the eight hundred years that Islam has been around in the sub-continent, Muslims have raised their hands to the Almighty, praised the Holy Prophet and punctiliously recited the Quran. But nothing in their creed, or their understanding of it has ever stopped them from enjoying and celebrating life.' Yes, celebration of life is exactly what the Taliban forbid."

Another very important shift related to the perception of Indian intentions in the grim situation obtaining in Pakistan. The myth of Indian aggressive territorial designs against Pakistan to "whose creation Hindus were never reconciled" perpetuated for six decades had since been exploded. The ISI chief Lt. Gen. Pasha himself told German Magazine *Der Spiegl* January last, "We may be crazy in Pakistan, but not completely out of our minds. We know full well that terror is our enemy, not India" Kamran Shafi summed up the commonly held view in his piece 'Cravenness every where' published in *Dawn* of 17 April. He wrote, "I may also point out here that, like a lot of us, I do not think there is any danger of an attack by India. I think India has its job cut out in trying to make the lives of its people better, in industrialising itself, in bringing in foreign investment and tourists. What they will be extremely worried about is the take-over of Pakistan by fanatics, however, just as we would be worried if Bal Thackeray and gang were to take over India. All they have to do if that happens is to reinforce their borders."

There were doubting toms, diehard India baiters and Taliban sympathisers ensconced in the power structure tactically biding their time. It should be hoped that the winds of change blowing across the Islamic republic of Pakistan will gain further momentum in days to come and develop the capacity to sweep away the debris of the past prejudices, misconceptions, follies and insecurities.

"What's our world-view?" queries Ajaz Amir in his Battle for Pakistan (Battle of Pakistan) published in *Dawn* and says,

"Let us not get *ensnared* in the metaphysics of something we have been unable to define since the blood-laden circumstances of our fitful birth. To come straight to the point, to win against the Frankenstein brigades created by our past follies — baptismal games at which our American friends played the role of Godfather — the Pakistani state in all its functions must perform better, and must be seen by the wretched of the earth (or rather the wretched of Pakistan) as a better alternative, than the Taliban." The core question is, will and can the forces now being marshalled against the Taliban in Pakistan successfully meet the twin challenges and achieve the goal?

PART III

16

Legacy of a Dictator

Dictator's Legacy

Tariq Fatemi in his perceptive article, "Self-appointed Messiahs *(Dawn*, 13 January, 2011) pertinently pointed out, "Though he was the fourth in the line of generals who violated their oaths as soldiers, he has the distinction of having done this more than once. Having overthrown an elected government, sent parliament packing and causing some political leaders to go into exile, he created an edifice based on duplicity. When it began to collapse, he once again violated the Constitution and its laws, muzzling the media, locking up members of civil society and attempting to sack the chief justice."

Convinced of his infallibility and powered by unbridled ambition, Musharraf did not hesitate to do violence to the vital institutions of Pakistan including his mother organisation – the Pakistan Army.

On assumption of power, he quickly and brutally "fixed" colleagues of decades who had dared not to fall in the line. Gen. Zia-ud-Din was humiliated and kept in solitary confinement in a tiny cell for the sin of having been appointed as Musharraf's successor by the competent authority. He was allowed exit from the country only after murmurs against the naked vendetta began to be reported from army jawans and officers Messes. By unceremoniously discarding his close associate Generals who stuck their necks out to install a dismissed Musharraf at the apex of the power structure in absentia out of sheer loyalty, he conclusively demonstrated his deceitful personality traits.

By mid June 2004, the rot that had set in the Pakistan army began to foul the environment. Under the caption 'Role of Pakistan Army Under Musharraf Just Stinks' Shaheen Sehbai (*South Asia Tribune* June13-19, 2004) wrote, "With the attacks on the army now becoming menacing by the day, Musharraf himself included, it is just a matter of time that anyone, just about anyone, wearing a military uniform will be attacked, if for nothing, just for the heck of it. This situation is becoming perilously similar to the weeks and months shortly after the fall of Dacca in 1971 when no army officer was comfortable coming out of his home in the *khaki*. The uniform had become an embarrassment and officers would not disclose their rank when asked to introduce themselves" This may be a somewhat harsh and extreme reading of the then prevailing situation but there was no doubt that the army under Musharraf had forfeited the popular reverence and fallen from the high pedestal on which the Pakistani nation had placed it since the creation of the country. According to Sehbai, *Asia Times Online*, "a credible source of insider stories about the army, has already reported that even a brigadier was killed a few months back as part of the failed bid to kill Musharraf. Many officers have been 'kidnapped' and pamphlets in military cantonments have become the popular mode of communication." This web-site also produced copy of a confidential GHQ Memo which speaks of 'special detention centres' where 'dozens' of officers and soldiers are being held without rights in extremely inhuman conditions. A copy of a handwritten letter by one Major Atta to the Government of Pakistan has been reproduced by the web-site as proof of the despicable situation of these dozens of detainees in special cells."

The write up went on, "He (Musharraf) was no visionary and no Kamal Ataturk, as he very proudly wanted to be. He was an insecure officer, thrown up by his faithful friends.

Basically he was a tin pot dictator who was soon to fall into the trappings of palace intrigues to keep him in power at any cost: political, moral, social, religious, national disintegration whatever." "It also accused him of stark nepotism" stating that "the next round of promotions (2004) to crucial corps commander slots that are planned are all close relatives of Musharraf, and his wife". 'The set up stinks' was the damning verdict".

Judiciary

To attain legitimacy for his regime, an indispensable requirement for a 'military takeover', Musharraf needed a 'captive' Supreme Court. He therefore, began his stint as the Chief Executive of Pakistan by restructuring the apex court to rid it of 'inconvenient and stubborn judges'. The Oath of Judges Order 2000 required the Judges to take a fresh oath of office swearing allegiance to military rule. Justice Iftikhar Chaudhry was one of the judges who dutifully took the fresh oath. The reshuffled Supreme Court validated the LFO Ordinance and gave the new Chief Executive no cause for complaint. All appeared to be well on the judicial front.

As his confidence level soared, Musharraf felt he could afford to experiment with an independent judiciary and free media. This would bolster up his image as a democrat and liberal, qualities which are endearing in the West especially the USA.

The problem with despots and dictators was that they failed to comprehend the primary natural instincts of freedom of thought and action as well as attributes of self-esteem embedded in the consciousness of every human being from the moment of conception in the womb. In real life, external environment and pressures of diverse nature, compulsions of ambition and weakness of character can and do succeed in suppressing these urges in vast majority of people. These, however, lie dormant waiting to assert at the right moment. What distinguishes man from the machine is that the former has a mind of his own that thinks and responds to different stimuli at different time and not necessarily in the same manner. So when Musharraf appointed Justice Iftikhar Choudhry as the Chief Justice of Supreme Court on 30 June, 2005, he did not realise that he was stoking a personality transformation. The status, prestige and authority that went with the job tickled natural instincts stored in the subconscious. The advent of independent phase of judiciary was to prove liberating.

A proactive stance adopted by the Supreme Court in petitions filed by the Human Rights Commission of Pakistan regarding150 missing persons ignited confrontation with the executive. Every time a missing person was produced in the court, accountability and credibility of the officials and legitimacy of the system came to be questioned and battered by the court.

An infuriated Musharraf summoned Iftikhar Muhammad Choudhry, the Supreme Court Chief Justice to the Army House on 9th of March, 2007. He was reported to have been accorded the standard treatment reserved for people fallen from favour and made to cool his heals in the reception area before being marched up to the President holding court with prime minister Shaukat Aziz and six other uniformed generals in attendance.

Apparently, it never occurred to a naive and power-drunk Musharraf that the enormous prestige and majesty of an independent judiciary did not terminate at the gates of the army house–the residence of the President of Pakistan. The humiliating wait instead of the intended 'softening' actually made the chief justice very angry. The line up of uniformed and bemedelled Generals and the prime minister intended to overawe only heightened the tension. Musharraf was, therefore, completely unprepared for the defiant response to his demand for resignation. The Chief Justice's refusal to oblige the President resulted in his being made 'non-functional'. The unprecedented development unleashed an equally unprecedented revolt by Pakistani lawyers in support of judicial independence and the rule of law. The 'Lawyers' Mutiny assumed the shape of widespread street action that predictably sucked in the people, the media and the politicians of different hues including Benazir Bhutto and Nawaz Sherif. What followed is history.

Reinstatement of Iftikhar Muhammad Chaudhary as the Chief Justice of Supreme Court of Pakistan and his companion judges marked the success of the movement and symbolised the assertion of an independence of judiciary. But at what cost? Whether Chief Justice Iftikhar Chaudhary climbed down from his high pedestal to turn an agitator due to compulsion of circumstances created by Musharraf and his administration or was attracted by mass adulation and the pleasing and exhilarating touch of fragrant rose petal showered by people in the streets, the value system, restraint, objectivity and impartiality which comprised the essence of justice delivery system and informed the judicial mindset took a very severe beating.

The ongoing 'contempt of court drama' about the central theme of prosecuting the President of the Islamic Republic of Pakistan in the courts of another democracy who like all heads of states in democracies enjoyed immunity from such actions was a case in point. The issue was addressed by Justice Markandey Katju, a former judge of Supreme Court of India, currently chairman, Press Council of India, in his article Pakistan's Supreme Court has gone Overboard *(Pannun Kashmir*, Jammu, June 23, 2012). Referring to Section 248(2) of Pakistan Constitution which states, "No criminal proceedings whatsoever shall be instituted, or continued against the President, or Governor in any court during his term of office," he points out that "the language of the provision is clear, and it was a settled principle of interpretation that when language was clear the court shall not twist, or amend its language in garb of interpretation but read it as it is." He also questioned the authority of the court to remove a prime minister who "held office as long he enjoyed the confidence of Parliament, not the confidence of Supreme Court". "It (the Pak SC) has clearly gone overboard and flouted all norms of constitutional jurisprudence."

A bench of the Pakistan Supreme Court surprised one and all by reeling out a list of options to the Federal Government integral to sphere of activity that roundly and squarely fall in the domain of the executive. Casting aside all restraints and even good manners an honourable judge of the Apex court passed undeserved derogatory (bordering on abusive) remarks against the then prime minister of the country in an open Court. The matters come to a pass that Judiciary was being perceived as an active player in the murky power game in Pakistan in partnership with the Pakistan Army.

Supreme Court of Pakistan seemed to be losing some of its sheen of dignity and sanctity. Take the case of the "Memogate" scandal in which music video featuring bikini-clad female wrestlers were cited as evidence of immorality on the part of the key witness Mansoor Ijaz making the court the arena for such lurid political theatre. "In the long run this is a very dangerous trend," said Muneer A. Malik, a former president of the Supreme Court Bar Association who campaigned for Justice Chaudhry in 2007. "The judges are not elected representatives of the people and they are arrogating power to themselves as if they are the only sanctimonious institution in the country. All dictators fall prey to this psyche — that only we are clean, and capable of doing the right thing" he concluded.

Musharraf currently in self-exile in London was a fugitive from justice. A 14 - Judge bench of Pakistan Supreme presided over by Chief Justice Iftikhar Choudhry declared the emergency promulgated by him (Musharraf) on Nov. 3, 2007 and the consequent dismissal of judges as unconstitutional. Also illegal were the Provisional Constitutional Order (PCO), the Emergency Law and appointments of judges made under it. It was further held that General Musharraf in his dual capacity as the Army Chief and the President had subverted the Constitution which amounted to Treason under article 6 of 1973

Constitution of Pakistan. The offence was punishable with death penalty or life imprisonment. A bench of the Sindh High Court directed the authorities to register a case against former military ruler Pervez Musharraf on charges of treason. Moreover an anti-terrorism court in Rawalpindi issued an arrest warrant for Musharraf for failing to cooperate with the FIA in its probe into the assassination of former premier Benazir Bhutto. A request by the Pakistan government to secure a Red Corner Warrant from Interpol has, however, not met with success so far as the evidence provided was considered insufficient by the Interpol.

A special anti-terrorism court (ATC) in Sibbi (Quetta) while hearing the murder case of Akbar Bugti, registered at the Kohlu Police Station issued arrest warrants against former president Pervez Musharraf, former prime minister Shaukat Aziz, Balochistan former chief minister Jam Mohammad Yousaf, Balochistan former governor Awais Ahmed Ghani and other accused nominated in the First Information Report. Arrest warrants were also issued for former interior minister Aftab Khan Sherpao. The court ordered that the accused be arrested and produced before it during the next hearing.

A vital pillar of the Islamic Republic appears to have been derailed, its values distorted and systemic restraints compromised. The roots of judicial waywardness and arbitrariness that afflict the august institution can be traced to attempts at manipulation and arms twisting resorted to by Dictator Parvez Musharraf.

Economy

Western economic analysts painted a rosy picture of the economy of Pakistan under Musharraf. Even the PPP led government was reported to have averred that the "Pakistan's economy witnessed a major economic transformation in the last decade. The country's real GDP increased from $60 billion to $170 billion, with per capita income rising from under $500 to over $1000 during 2000-07". It further acknowledged that "the volume of international trade increased from $20 billion to nearly $60 billion. The improved macroeconomic performance enabled Pakistan to re-enter the international capital markets in the mid-2000s. Large capital inflows financed the current account deficit and contributed to an increase in gross official reserves to $14.3 billion at end-June 2007. Buoyant output growth, low inflation, and the government's social policies contributed to a reduction in poverty and improvement in many social indicators (MEFP, November 20, 2008, Para 1). If all this be true then what did the PPP government do to so quickly impoverish the country's economy and bring it to the brink of collapse in record time.

The answer was provided by Dr. Subhash Kapila an International Relations and Strategic Affairs analyst and Consultant, Strategic Affairs with South Asia Analysis Group in his write up, Pakistan-A Reality Check on Five Years of Army Rule (2004). According to him, "Pakistan's economic indicators stand fudged by the United States post 9/11 in order to justify the American strategic expediency General Musharraf's continuance as military ruler of Pakistan to serve American strategic interests in the region." Actually American financial *largesse* has flowed into Pakistan in billions of American dollars post 9/11 enabling the balancing of cash registers. Minus the American largesse, Pakistan is still a failed state. "In terms of social indicators", he added, "even basic infrastructure in the fields of health and education have not made its presence felt in the last five years". Pakistani children have to seek medical treatment in India facilitated by relaxation of visas by India. Madarsas, the infrastructure and nursery of Islamic Jehad still flourish in thousands as the Pakistan Army is yet to provide alternative education to Pakistan's impoverished masses,' he added

The Rand Corporation's Seth Jones said the army occupies a unique spot in Pakistan's society. And had for decades. "The Pakistani army", Jones told *Kai Ryssdal,* "is not just involved in defence but it also has quite a complex conglomerate. You know most of these small scale and large scale corporate enterprises range from private security firms and bakeries, farms, schools, to insurance companies to cement and cereal manufacturing plants" (Seth Jones interviewed by *Kai Ryssdal,* Nov. 6, 2007). According to some estimates, Pakistan's army controls businesses worth as much as $40 billion. May be 10 per cent of the whole economy.

An affordable and easy access to consumer goods and the quality of life an average citizen enjoyed were true barometers of the health of an economy. Judged by this yardstick, Pakistan during Musharraf's rule was an prolonged nightmare. It was literally a dark period. The common man kept on groping in the dark and howling for "Bijli", which rarely made an appearance and even when it did appear played hide and seek. 'Atta' (wheat flour), the staple diet of a Pakistani disappeared from government ration shops and the market, but was available in abundance in the black market run by politicians in power and their minions. Musharraf's government for reasons which were suspect exported wheat, the critical commodity, which certainly was not surplus to country's own requirements in 2007, thereby creating artificial shortages resulting in avoidable price hike. And when hungry, disillusioned and distraught people made common cause with the agitating lawyers swelling their ranks, the PML (Q) government had to pack up and go. So did Musharraf little later then.

Women Emancipation

Musharraf's contribution to women empowerment in the state power structure in the prevailing socio-religious environment in Pakistan should have qualified him for a place of honour in the history. He was responsible for taking to revolutionary step of enhancing the number of reserved seats for women in assemblies – from 20 to 60 in the national and 128 seats in provincial assemblies. The impact of this very significant reform was reflected in 2008 elections which recorded substantial increase in participation of women as compared to 1988 polls. But this was not to be. His concern for women rights was soon exposed as fake. His worst kind of made chauvinistic pronouncement of Captain Hammad, accused of rape of Dr. Shazia Khalid, a physician working on a government gas plant in Baluchistan as innocent even before the judicial inquiry concluded completed exposed him *Times,* (2005-03-04).

The Bugti tribal tradition viewed the rape in their heartland as a breach of their code of honour. The reaction was particularly sharp and violent as the rapist happened to be an officer of the hated Pak army. Tribesmen went on the rampage and attacked the gas plant. An arrogant and vengeful dictator responded by sending tanks, helicopters and reinforcement of almost five army battalions to secure the installation and 'teach Bugti tribesmen a lesson.' If the tribesmen failed to stop shooting, he warned on television, "they will not know what hit them". Shazia, the victim was compelled by the Pakistan government to leave the country. (*The Guardian,* 21 February, 2005).

Musharraf had taken the Shazia affair almost personally. Throwing all caution to winds, he made the astounding statement to the *Washington Post* in an interview in September 2005 that Pakistani women victims in Pakistan treated rape as a 'moneymaking concern' and were only interested in the publicity in order to make money and get a Canadian visa. He subsequently denied having made the comments. The *Washington Post*, however, pricked the balloon of his assertion by producing an audio recording of the interview, in which Musharraf could be heard making the above quoted remarks (*Washingtonpost.com.* 2005-09-23). Remark made by Musharraf sparked outrage and protests at home and abroad.

Another Pakistani rape victim, Mukhtaran Mai was denied the right to travel abroad. Ultimately Musharraf had to relent under pressure by US State Department and grant the permission.

The Trait of Duplicity

Musharraf's management of affairs of Pakistan followed the classical pattern of hunting with the hound and running with the hare. Post–9/11, he jumped on the US led anti-terrorist band wagon but tasked the ISI to maintain strategic and political relations with the Taliban. It could not and did not remain a secret for too long. If American suffered him despite being aware of his treachery, they had and still have their own compulsions.

When Tehrik-e-Taliban, another ISI surrogate became active in Waziristan in support of the Afghan Taliban fighting US led NATO forces and the United States called for stern action against them. In fact, American outsourced the job of subduing Pakistani Taliban operating on the Pakistan side of Pak-Afghan border to Pak army. Musharraf agreed to perform the task which included safe passage to transportation by road of Military supplies to NATO forces fighting Taliban in Afghanistan for a price. Consequently, Pakistan received assistance under the "coalition support funds" (CSF) a mounting to $8.9 billion as May 2011. The amount equals roughly one-fifth to one-quarter of Pakistan's total military expenditures during this period. Still he double-timed the Americans, and Pakistan continued to do so despite the fact that the shadow-boxing scripted by Musharraf had since become a live combat between TTP powered by Al-Qaeda ideology and Pak army. Thousands of lives have been lost and lakhs of people dislocated. Tehrik-e-Taliban Pakistan has since forged alliance with other Sunni extremist groups like Lashkar-e-Jhangvi and extended its reach to all nooks and corners of the country. The Tehrik has humiliated Pakistan army by successfully targeting sensitive defence installations. No one is by now left in doubt about the aim of the TTP terrorist to seize power in Islamabad.

"We must understand the nature of this war. It is not between two armies. It is between two world-views and unless the world-view that the Pakistani state seemingly stands for is more powerful and makes more sense, the Taliban will win and the Pakistani state, as represented by its increasingly decrepit administrative machinery, will lose, "warned Ayaz Amir" in his *'Islamabad Diary'* (Battle for Pakistan).

"The Battle for Pakistan will not be won, and the Taliban not eventually defeated, if the culture of luxury and undue privilege at the top of the military— a culture symbolised by the multiplicity of residential plots appropriated by the topmost ranks — is not drastically curtailed". "In short" he wrote, *"braid, and too much brass, and luxury limos and generals acquiring,* while still in service, the mentality of real estate agents is no way to fight the Taliban and rescue Pakistan from the predicament into which it is slipping." (*Islamabad diary* by Ayjaz Amir, *Dawn* May, 2009).

Irfan Husain addressed the other dimension– the alienation of the people and the intelligentsia from the army in his recent article, 'The widening gulf' he wrote "I have never seen the level of anger towards the military and the intelligence that is presently evident in the media and on the Internet. Normally, this is Pakistan's holiest of sacred cows. However, in a recent broadcast, I saw Kamran Khan, the popular TV host otherwise seen as sympathetic to the military establishment, hold forth about the recent terrorist attack at the Mehran naval base in Karachi. After describing the event, he went on to remind the sacrifices Pakistan had made to keep senior officers comfortable, detailing the plots they received, as well as their value. He also showed viewers a shot of the bullet-proof BMW Series - 7 limousine at the navy chief's disposal. According to him, the car is worth Rs. 500 m to Rs. 600 m. Similar models have been handed out to all corps commanders."

Ever since Taliban militancy erupted in Waziristan, a perception was foisted in the national mindset that Pakistanis were being made to kill fellow Muslims to serve aggressive designs of hated Americans. The army was fightig against their own people because it was obliged to carry out orders as a disciplined force. Sane voices like that of Ayjaz Amir drawing attention to fundamental issues were waved away as intellectual acrobats. This attitude appears to be changing. There are indeed signs of recognition of the serious threat to the very existence of the Islamic Republic of Pakistan from within "Gen. Kayani and his institution may have taken their time getting here but it is refreshing to hear the army chief say that those who seek to impose their 'flawed' thinking using the force of arms, those who threaten our way of life, must be stopped by a united front", says Abbas Nasir, former editor of *Dawn* in his write up 'Fight to Finish' (*Dawn* 18 August, 2012). General Kayani's statement is reminiscent of the speech delivered by him to the 118 Corpse commanders conference in Rawalpindi on 07 May 2009. Expressing the military's resolve to fight and eliminate the militants endangering the lives of peaceful citizens and challenging the writ of the state. Kayani, had then also urged national harmony to fight terrorism, extremism. "The present security situation requires that all elements of national power should work in close harmony to fight the menace of terrorism and extremism" he maintained. This is exactly what an army chief was expected to say. It did not necessarily express his conviction. The latest statement, on the other hand, reflected correct interpretation of the blood soaked ground realities and recognition of the theocratic engine that drove the 'flawed thinking'. Its imposition by force is clearly integral to fundamentalist fanaticism capable of being expressed only through violence and terror. Of enormous significance, however, was his Aug. 14 address to the gathering at the Pakistan Military Academy, Kabul, where in he warned that "any disagreement on how to deal with the militant threat could be the potential trigger for a civil war." The danger is real and the threat imminent.

General Kiyani is a very worried man. He heads a military machine which constitutes and harbours many who support the imposition of the "flawed thinking by using force of arms". Then there are proxies like Difa-e-Pakistan Council (DPC) and ideological allies like Pakistan Tehrik-e-Insaf chief, Imran Khan. "The one intangible troubling, some analysts say, is whether some 'surrogates' such as the DPC and ideological allies such as the PTI chief may now have so cemented the thinking that was promoted to serve a temporary purpose that they may not be amenable to change" (*Dawn,* 18 August, 2012).

Given the composition of DPC, the General will have to tread cautiously, but be sure that he does not shy away from taking suitable pre-emptive action if circumstances so demand. As far as political class is concerned the ruling coalition will come aboard without any reservation. It may take some time and effort to convince Nawaz Sharef. Of course, General Kiyani would know that in the situation that prevails, unity of only like minded is necessary as well as desirable. Everyone has to choose his/her side. The Pakistani nation can not afford to continue the 'whose war' sterile debate any further. The stakes are too high to admit of any further delay or experimentation.

Musharraf departed from the Aiwan-e-Sadder leaving the nation-state hovering on the brink of ultimate disaster. A state of near anarchy prevailed throughout the country. There were serious question marks on capability of Pakistan establishment to secure its nuclear assets. This was causing lot of concern in world capitals. Military strategists the world over were busy considering various options to secure Pak nuclear assets whatever the cost.

All vital institutions including Pakistan army were fractured and subverted. The nation was at war with itself, what with Tehrik-e-Taliban, an illegitimate and wayward off spring of ISI indulging in senseless killings and menacingly knocking at the doors of Islamabad and sectarian violence tearing the Muslim society asunder. The intensification of revolt in strategically sensitive Balochistan and enhanced interest that USA China and Iran evinced in that theatre stoked fears of secession of the largest and strategically important province of Pakistan which was endowed with enormous natural resource. Number of regional and other powers eye Gowader, the sole warm water port in the region constructed and controlled by Chinese government who have comprehensively linked it with their own and Pakistani economic and strategic assets.

"Musharraf's departure is certainly a watershed that brings to an end a long period of personalised military rule. However, the mess, he has left behind, is one that will haunt Pakistan and the world in the months ahead and make the international community even more nervous about the future of Pakistan as the militants become stronger and more audacious" (Ahmed Rashid, *Telegraph*, 19 August, 2008).

Ahmed Rashid was being unduly conservative. Four years down the line, the vital state institutions are still reeling under the pernicious and debilitating Musharraf effect. With a judiciary run amok, the government in doledrums and prospects of civil war looming large before a conflict ridden nation, its future, to put it mildly can not but be uncertain. So where does Pakistan go from here? The prospective scenario raises many other vital issues.

Will elements across the politico-religious-military spectrum committed to stop the imposition of "flawed thinking by force and threatening the way of life" General Kayani has spoken about unite to take on the bad guys? How much and what kind of support the world community will provide them in the conflict, the outcome whereof will impact not only the South Asia but the entire world? And if shove comes to push and the pro fundamentalist segment in the Pakistan army break rank signalling the start of civil war, what about the security of Pakistan nuclear assets? What will the USA and other countries worried sick about such an eventuality do to secure these critical assets? More importantly, what contingency plans does India have to pre-empt such a disastrous development and how deeply and intimately are these hooked into those of the USA and other concerned countries? Answers — pragmatic and practical for these and many other questions have to be found, or crafted on topmost priority. While Pakistan's neighbouring countries and the world community mull over the responses to the serious threats to the civilised way of life, one wonders if disgraced Dictator of Pakistan, former General Musharraf ensconced in his luxurious quarters away from the heat of Islamabad even realises how much trouble has been caused by his commandos washbuckling and insane duplicity to his mother organisation, the Pakistan army, Pakistan and indeed the entire world community. In fact, the double speaking antics of the self-proclaimed protagonist of moderate Islam ended up acting as force multiplier for the likes of Al Qaeda and Talban thereby significantly enhancing the threat to a civilised world order and peace.

The political dimension of General's role in politics and governance in Pakistan by now an integral party of country's political system, was engaging the attention of intellectuals and analysts. I found the following perspective of Dr. Hassan Askari, Rizvi an eminent Pakistani political and defence analyst *Times* October 15, 2012), both relevant and thought provoking.

"Political failures facilitate assumption of power by generals but military regimes are unable to remedy the weaknesses of social and political processes and institutions. Military regimes are part of the problems that cause political degeneration and decay and are viewed as a major obstacle to developing viable participatory institutions and processes. The political institutions they set up reflect management rather than participatory perspectives and cannot accommodate participatory pressures in a diversified society. "It makes lot of sense. But democracy has to take firm roots in Pakistan if Generals are to be kept at bay and dissuaded from subverting constitution and usurping political power.

Ousted from power, Musharraf tried to put up a brave face but public hostility, fear of criminal prosecution and impeachment by National assembly and above all the realisation that the army would not bat for him beyond a point opted for self-exile in London and Dubai. For last about five years he kept himself busy issuing statements, managing TV interviews and delivering lectures, in which he routinely threatened to return to Pakistan, like all ousted dictators, Musharraf had convinced himself of his ever enduring popularity in Pakistan, indispensability for the country and political invincibility.

As the elections approached, Pakistan found herself in the throes of grave political, economic and governance crisis. Scandals were galore, governance touched a new low and its three vital institutions-the Supreme court, the parliament/ Federal government and army locked horns on issues of prosecution of President Zardari on corruption charges in Court in Switzerland, accountability of Pakistan army to civilian authority of democratically elected government/parliament and me issue of "Missing persons" allegedly whisked away by the ISL There was even talk of Military intervention, The Army, however sensibly called "no bid".

The announcement of the schedule for elections effectively sidetracked the elements of crisis. The election fever took hold. But ensconced in his luxurious quarters away from the heat of Islamabad and living in a make believe world, Musharraf perceived himself as the Messiah mat Pakistan needed and awaited Brushing aside not so subtle hints from the army, he boarded a plane in Dubai with supporters and journalists in style which brought him to Karachi airport on March, 24, 2013. Hisreturn was aimed at staging a political comeback despite Taliban death threats and looming arrest warrants. But to his surprise and shock only couple of thousands people turned out to receive him and his party at the airport despite elaborate preparations and financial investment. "Musharraf evidently overestimated his popularity," commented Raza Rumi, a political analyst. "He ruled on the strength of his uniform".

"Now that uniform has gone, and Pakistan has changed." The man who boasted he would out-Benazir the Bhutto in popular support was shunned by even those who had benefited during his illegitimate and undemocratic regime. Compared to the political colossus that Banazir in deed was, Mushaaraf turned out to be a mere pygmy. Still he kept up the facade. "I have put my life in danger and have come to Pakistan— to you to be the saviour of this country," he declared at Karachi airport.

The subsequent developments revealed that the smart Commando had walked into a trap. To ward off a potential arrest, Mushaaraf had taken pre-emptive measures by securing bail in advance of his arrival to Pakistan. "We have made sure that he is not arrested and his return home will be smooth," said Jawed Siddiqui, a member of the former president's party, True, but what there after ? It was conveniently forgotten that by humiliating and incarcerating the Chief justice of the Supreme court and his brother judges and committing atrocities on lawyers and the intelligentsia Musharraf had made powerful enemies. They were around very angry and determined to make him pay for his sins. Only mass support might have operated as restraining factor but it never was there. Moreover as one commentator put it" At the age of 69, his swaggering days are done".

His bail was revoked in a case involving his decision to fire senior judges while in power over five years ago. The Man, who when questioned by a prominent anchor on an Indian TV channel whether he had entered Indian territory in Kargil during conflict proudly declared "I always lead from the front" sneaked away from the court like...whatever?. Finally arrested, Mushaarai was taken to Police HQRS where he was kept overnight perhaps to teach him the lesson of equality before law. The former Dictator was now confined in his Farm House which was 'graciously' declared a "sub-jail" by the authorities Tense and demoralised, he awaits the conclusion of cases ranging from murder to Sedition which could sent him to jail for life. The rejection of all four nomination papers for National Assembly seats filed by him by Election authorities shattered of what was left of his dreams. While Mushaaraf was busy courting trouble or wrestling with problems of his own creation, a democratically elected government completed its full term for the first time in Pakistan's history. Power was gracefully transferred to the Care Taker government as mandated by its constitution. Elections were held in which abut 53 per cent electorate cast their votes defying terrorist threats and ignoring targeted killings. Unmindful of the tense environment and blood shed Young men and women marched to polling booths raising slogans and dancing turning the poll day into a festival of democracy. This grand assertion of preference for, nay commitment to democracy was great news for Pakistan and foretold her bright future. Elections over, the new democratic dispensation headed by Nawaz Sherif whose Muslim League(N) enjoys a comfortable majority in the parliament and whom Mushaaraf had overthrown in a treacherous coup and jailed has since taken over and formed the government. From here Mushaaraf s troubles can only increase. Whatever fate befalls Mushaaraf, it appears that days of Army rule in Pakistan are over.

Index

C